the Chain Saw Craft Book

by
Harold C. MacIntosh

© 1980 By Harold C. MacIntosh

All rights reserved, including those to reproduce this book, or parts thereof, in any form, without permission in writing from the Publisher.

Library of Congress Cataloging in Publication Data

MacIntosh, Harold C. 1940–
 The chain saw craft book.

  1. Power tools. 2. Chain saws. I. Title.
TT153.5.M33   621.9'3   79-26113
ISBN 0-87108-516-X

First Edition
   2 3 4 5 6 7 8 9

Printed in the United States of America

All photographs and drawings were provided by the author.

Illustrative material appearing on pages 40-41 relating to the Granberg Mini-Mill reproduced through the courtesy of Granberg Industries, Richmond, California.

Contents

Introduction	1
1. Considerations in Choosing Wood	3
2. Obtaining Wood	5
3. General Procedures and Safety	7
4. How To	17
5. Projects	43
6. Log Structures	93
7. Trail and Camp	113
8. Farm and Ranch	121
9. Author's Background With Chain Saws	133

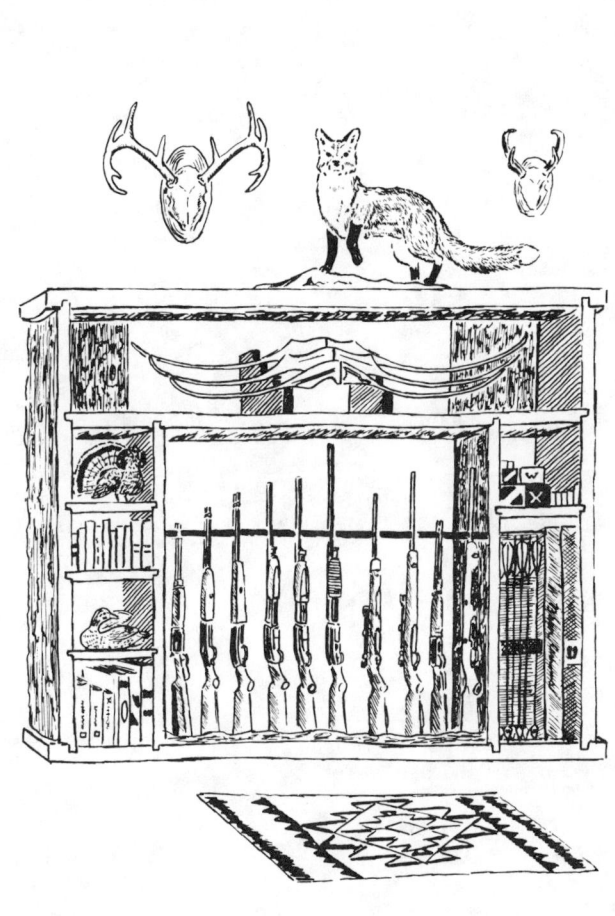
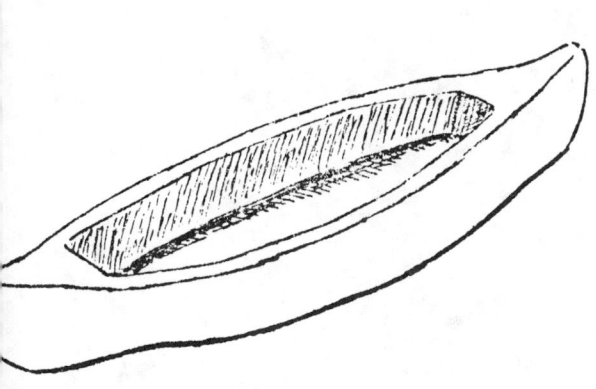

Introduction

The chain saw is a marvelous tool and one whose popularity has increased dramatically in recent years. The advent of new, lightweight models in a variety of sizes, at reasonable prices makes the chain saw an excellent investment.

This book is intended to supplement the obvious uses of the chain saw by suggesting ideas for new projects which will help you realize the full potential of your investment, and utilize scrap wood that might otherwise end up in the dump.

The projects described on the following pages will, it is hoped, add another dimension to your chain saw activities. Not only will you be able to put your saw to constructive new uses, but you will have hours of fun building these projects.

Good cutting. . . .

Harold C. MacIntosh

1.
Considerations in Choosing Wood

There are many factors in choosing wood. I suggest that you begin with dead, standing soft conifers or, if unavailable, the Poplar family of deciduous trees. Softer conifers are preferable, because of the ease in cutting and lightness in handling.

The size and toughness of the tree you work with will depend largely on the length of the bar and chain of your saw; the chain's sharpness, straightness of the bar, and the power of the saw. When working with dried conifers, there are not many chain saws which, when sharp and properly tuned, won't do just about anything—providing you don't force them and your bar is long enough.

If you live in the northeast and start to make your first piece of furniture with a fifty-five inch White Oak, or a sixty-inch American Elm, chances are you will lose interest quickly. So start out slow, using soft wood and save the hard stuff for later.

2.
Obtaining Wood

Some of us are fortunate enough to have just about any type and size of wood we want in our back yards, or in neighboring woods, where permission can be obtained to cut what is needed. For those who do not have wood so readily available, here are some suggestions.

Contact the local tree surgeon or trimmer. Describe your needs and ask him to drop a load of his cuttings in your yard the next time he is working in the neighborhood. You will probably acquire a little extra brush this way, but it can be used in the fireplace. The little extra effort is well worthwhile.

Another source is your local firewood dealer. Be prepared to pay for his time and equipment; however unlike the professional tree man, he never loads wood just to take to the dump.

Perhaps there is a dead tree in your neighborhood. If located on private property, ask the owner to have part of the tree dumped in your yard when and if it is removed. If the tree is owned by a state or local agency, such as the highway department or the department of city parks, you can contact them and request to have some of the wood when the tree is cut.

Another good source is the local dump. Very often, dumps will keep wood and brush separate from other forms of refuse, thus providing free and easy access to a wood supply.

If you are unable to obtain wood by any of the above methods, you can contact loggers, sawmills, conservation officers and county extension agents; any of whom will be happy to direct you to a source of supply.

Never trespass on private property, even when it appears to be an abandoned wood dump, without first obtaining permission. Most property owners will be more than happy to trade favors, but do not expect them to go out of their way to lose time and money, not to mention good firewood.

I once caught two men stealing wood on my Dad's place. I took them to my Dad, who is normally a nice, sociable type. The men claimed they did not know who the property owner was, but said they had tried to find out in order to obtain permission. This made Dad angry. He had owned the land longer than the combined ages of both trespassers, and everyone in town knew Dad owned this land. The point here is, don't try and pull the wool over some old rancher's eyes, or he'll lift your hide but good.

3.
General Procedures and Safety

Read the operation manual that comes with your chain saw. If you do not have a manual, your dealer should be able to provide you with a copy, or you can write directly to the manufacturer.

Never use an obviously defective, worn down, or sharpened down chain. If you do attempt to use a chain with teeth that are less than one quarter their original length, it is possible that a tooth might fly off and lodge in your face. Discard these old worn chains and obtain new ones.

When boring holes in logs and making plunge cuts, hold the saw firmly and run slowly until the tip of the bar is deep enough into the log so that it will not buck or slip out of the hole.

Be sure the rackers on the chain are not filed down beyond the manufacturer's prescribed recommendation. If they are filed down too far for this type of cutting, the chain will dig in the wood too severely and will cause lack of control of the saw.

When carving, hollowing, or planing logs, be sure the piece is firmly secured. One way to accomplish this is to cut or carve the project while it is still attached to the log, then cut the piece off when the job is nearly completed. Another method is to leave excess on one end of your project and spike it down to a suitable log or stump by this excess until the project is completed.

The following are a few safety procedures accompanied by cartoons:

1. Start saws properly. Be sure your saw is on a solid surface and that you have a solid position before starting your saw. Be careful of yourself and others.

2. Never cut beyond the hinge when felling a tree. As soon as you do, you lose control.

3. Never allow anyone within reaching or falling distance of you and your saw while it is running.

4. Make sure that the tree to be felled has plenty of clearance before starting to cut. Never allow spectators or pets within a falling or break up radius of any tree you are in the process of felling. Stay alert to the possibility of mobilized obstructions entering your work area.

5. Keep a clean work site.

6. Inspect all tools and equipment periodically. Sledge hammers and axes should be checked for loose or cracked handles; wedges should be checked for burrs that might break off and lodge in your eyes; gas cans checked for leaks; saws checked for tight screws and bolts.

7. Always check your footing before you take a step with a running saw.

8. Check standing trees for cracks and splits before felling.

9. Stay alert to natural conditions. Such as: natural lean of a tree, the weight distribution of the limbs and foliage, wind conditions and direction, loose, dead limbs (from the tree you are cutting or other trees in the area) that might fall when the tree is felled.

10. Be careful of bar tip kickback.

11. If your chain should stop turning, due to lack of lubrication, or if your bar and sprocket become clogged with wood chips, never try to clear it while the motor is still running.

12. If you should find occasion to use a fall rope, be sure it is longer than the tree is tall.

13. Be careful with push poles. If you are using a push pole, pike pole, or crotched stick for pushing over a tree, be sure that you and the pole are stout enough and that you have a good bite on the tree to be cut.

Felling a Tree in an Unrestricted Area

Cut a notch perpendicular to the desired direction of the fall. The notch should be one-third to one-quarter of the distance through on a sound tree. Horizontal and oblique cuts should meet clearly and evenly. One cut should not pass the other.

Make felling cut about two inches above the horizontal surface of the notch. Never extend felling cut beyond the hinge. Once the cut passes the hinge, the tree may fall in any direction regardless of the pull lines.

In many cases after the tree is notched and the felling cut has been made, as the tree starts to tip, the person making the felling cut can take slight corrective aiming measures. By watching the top of the tree and leaving more hinge on the desired side of the cut, the fall line can be adjusted.

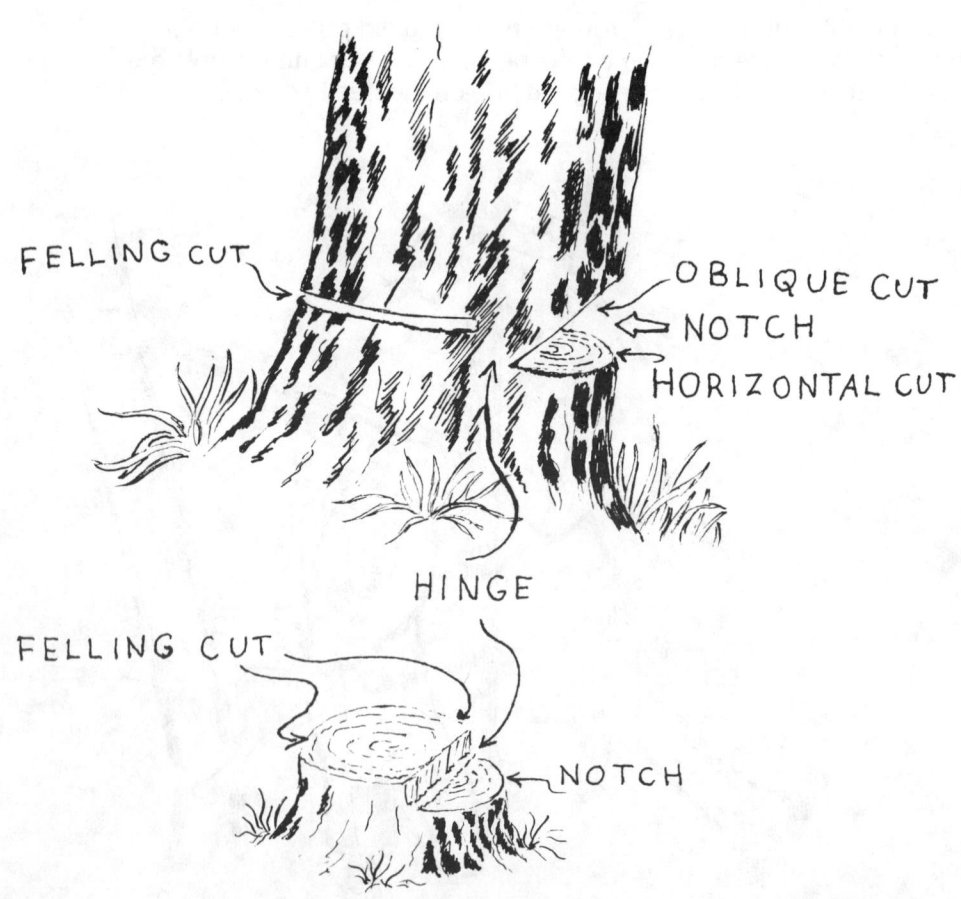

4.

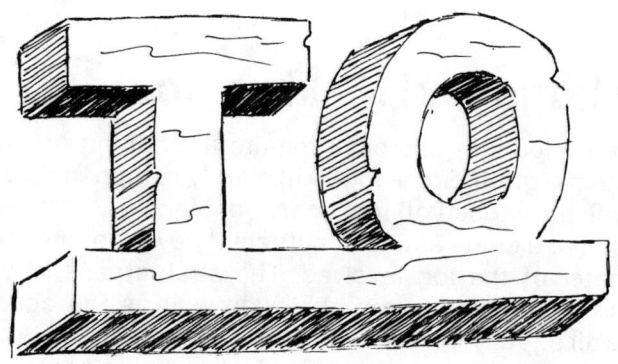

In this chapter I will cover all of the fundamental skills necessary for making most of the projects in this book.

I will show how to make notches, grooves and slots, square and rectangular holes, round holes and curved cuts. I will also explain how to rip logs and make boards, how to line up inserts, and how to plane with your chain saw, as well as large and small area hollowing.

Although much of this information will be repeated throughout the book as part of the instruction on a particular project, I recommend that you read this chapter carefully. The more familiar you become with these basic skills, the more you will be able to concentrate on the project at hand.

Ripping Logs and Making Boards

Many of the projects in this book require the ripping or cutting of logs long ways, with the grain. Some logs will merely be ripped down the center, while others will be slabbed off into boards or planks.

Ripping requires a chain saw with sufficient power for the species of tree and the diameter of the log involved. The straightness of your bar, the sharpness and condition of your chain, as well as the condition of the chain oiler are all equally important in obtaining a clean, smooth rip.

When ripping a log that can be moved by hand, it is best to set it on log cross braces, high enough to prevent the tip of the bar from touching the ground when the saw is tipped straight down. Before you begin, be sure the log is well braced to prevent rolling. If the log is too large to move by hand, try rolling it up on top of smaller logs, so it is firmly braced and high enough to prevent damage to the chain and bar.

If you wish to rip a fifty-five inch log with a forty inch bar, and only need a board forty inches wide for your project, you can accomplish this by first ripping off two sides of the log, being sure to leave forty inches across the middle. The log should then be rolled onto supports so that it rests on one of its flat sides. From this position you can then easily rip off the two remaining sides.

Now, using a chalk line, mark the desired thickness and cut the finished board.

When making these long rip cuts, you will occasionally have long, stringy pieces of sawdust. Periodically, you should stop the saw and clean out this sawdust. Also remove the large piles of sawdust from the cutting area. The amount of sawdust produced will depend greatly upon the species of tree being cut, the dryness or wetness of the wood and the condition of your chain.

Those who do not have an abundance of wood or the time to practice ripping lumber, may wish to consider investing in a chain saw Mini-Mill and ripping chains.

Planing

Planing is accomplished by idling the chain saw over the piece, gently at first, until you get the feel of handling the saw in this manner.

Maintain a firm grip on the saw and keep it gliding from side to side, to prevent actually cutting down into the wood. Planing is most easily done when the piece is on a table or other flat surface at elbow height. This makes the process less tiring and is a very comfortable working position.

Attempting to plane with the grain, especially on large, flat surfaces, is not recommended. The saw will tend to dig down deeper in the softer places and ride over the harder ones.

The drawing shows the fanning motion used to work out the worst of the grooves, and the sweeping motion used to smooth out final blemishes.

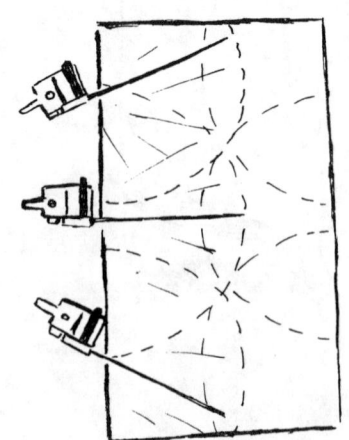 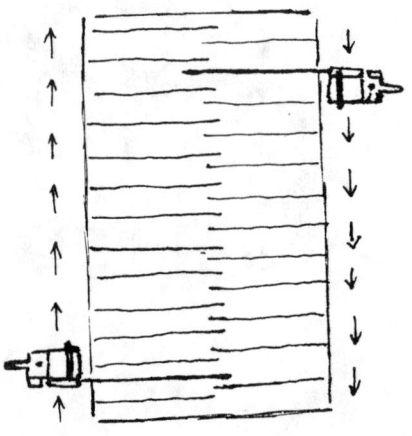

Square and Rectangular Holes

Square and rectangular holes are made by plunge cuts, using your narrowest bar and least powerful chain saw.

Running the saw at a slow idle, and at a slight angle to the piece, make the first two cuts perpendicular to the grain. Then make two plunge cuts with the grain to complete the square hole outline. Now make two more plunge cuts to form an X inside the square. Finally, make two plunge cuts to form a cross inside the X and square. The inside of the square can now be knocked out with hammer, mallet, or the back of your axe. If the hole is not deep enough, use the tip of the bar to grind out the hole to the desired depth.

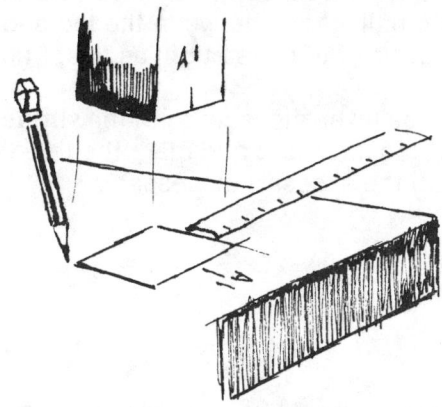

Plunge cuts used for boring holes through fence posts and similar items are also achieved by using your least powerful chain saw with the narrowest bar. Cutting with the grain and holding the saw at a lowered angle to the piece, begin to plunge through the log. After penetrating an inch and a half or more, increase the acceleration, if desired. Remember to keep a firm grip on both handles of the saw. After making the two outside cuts, running with the grain, make a series of plunge cuts inside the two outside cuts. You may wish to make an X-plunge cut within the rectangle. After making the necessary cuts, strike the wafers inside the hole at an angle (long ways), with a hammer or mallet to remove the wood in the center of the hole. To shape the hole, stick the bar through the hole. Run the saw back and forth at idle speed, chipping out the undesired rough edges.

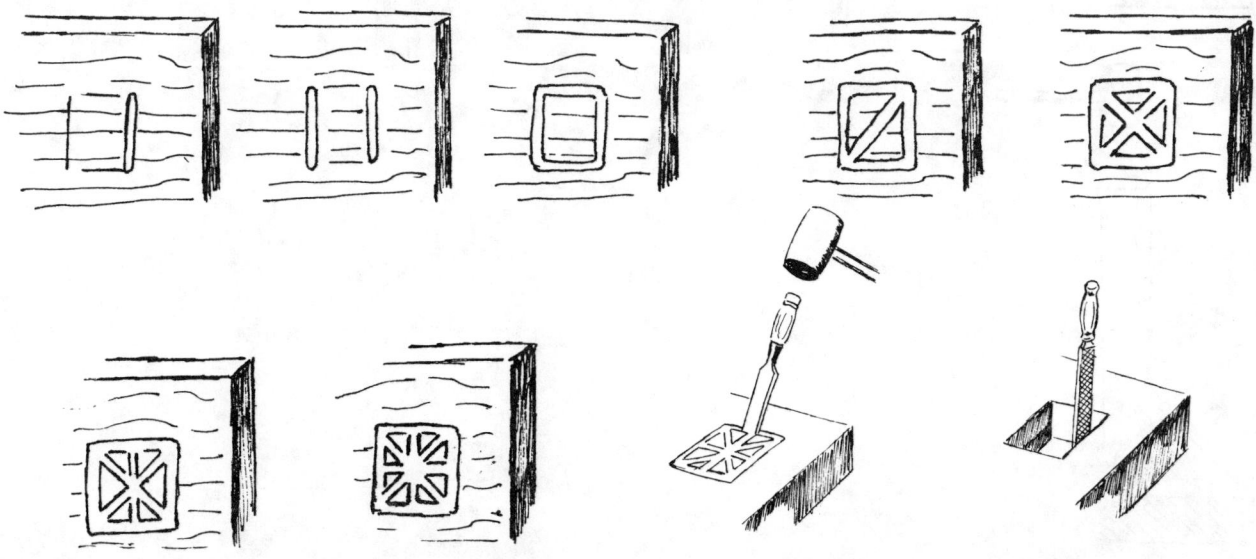

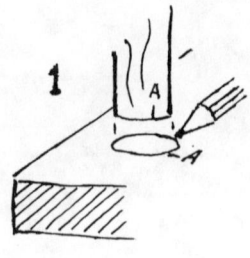
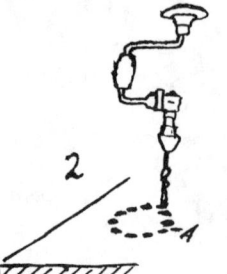
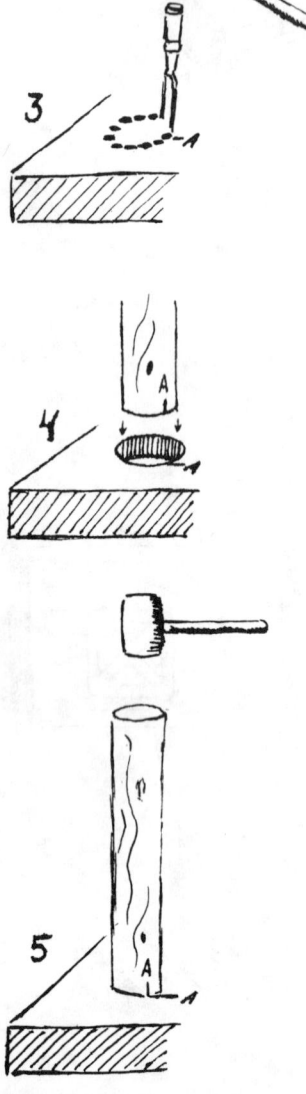

Round Holes

The procedure for making round holes in a table or bench top is relatively simple. Place the piece on the ground with the best side facing down. Cut and peel four small logs, of proportionate diameter and length for the project. Then mark each leg and hole separately, as no two legs will be exactly the same shape or diameter. This will make assembly easier later.

Drill holes two-thirds the thickness of the table top all the way around the pattern for each leg hole. Using a chisel or gouge, and mallet, remove the excess wood from inside the drilled out rings.

Line up the marks on the legs with the corresponding marks on the table top. Check for proper fit by inserting the legs with hand pressure. If the holes are too small, use a round sided wood rasp to enlarge the hole. If the holes are slightly large, insert a small wedge between the leg and wall of the hole. The tighter the fit, the better—but not so tight as to split the table top.

To insure that the table top will be level, measure from the surface of the top to the bottom of the shortest leg. Measure and mark the three remaining legs at the same height. Cut off the excess, if necessary.

Slots and Grooves

Using a pencil or crayon, trace the top of each leg on the bottom of the table, then mark each leg and the bottom of the table for ease in alignment when assembling.

Make a series of cuts close together, inside the outlined leg slot. If you are unable to remove all of the wood inside the slot with your chain saw, it may be necessary to use a chisel and mallet. Check slots for equal depth and leg fit, then make any necessary adjustments.

With the table top still upside down, drill two half-inch holes in each leg slot for dowel holes, being careful not to damage the table top by drilling too deeply. Damage can be prevented by placing a board tightly against the other side of the table top, where the drill will emerge.

Line up the marks on the table legs and the table slots and insert the legs.

Lay a heavy flat piece of wood across the bottom of the legs and drive them into place, using a mallet or hammer. Turn the table right side up and drill down in the dowel holes. Insert the dowels and cut flush with a hand saw.

SIDE VIEW

TOP VIEW

OPEN END

CLOSED END

Slots with Closed Ends

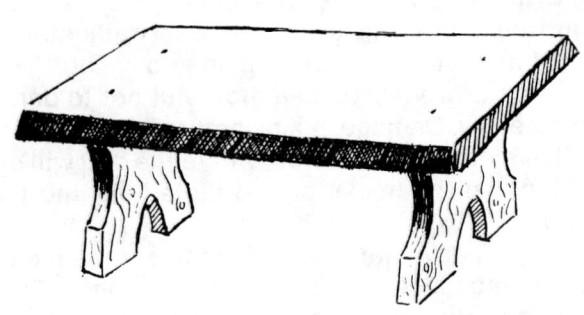

Notches

One method of making notches is to make a series of cuts, close together, at the desired depth of the notch. Make as many cuts as necessary for the width, then knock out the thin wafers with a hammer or an axe. In very hard woods, you may wish to use a mallet and chisel to remove the wafers. After the wafers have been removed, plane off the rough inside edges with your chain saw.

When making wide notches, such as used in linking a cabin, or in a book holder, it is sometimes more expedient to first make two side cuts the desired width of the notch. Then make the bottom cut by plunging the bar through the log, between the outside cuts, and perpendicular to them. Finally, cut to each side from the middle.

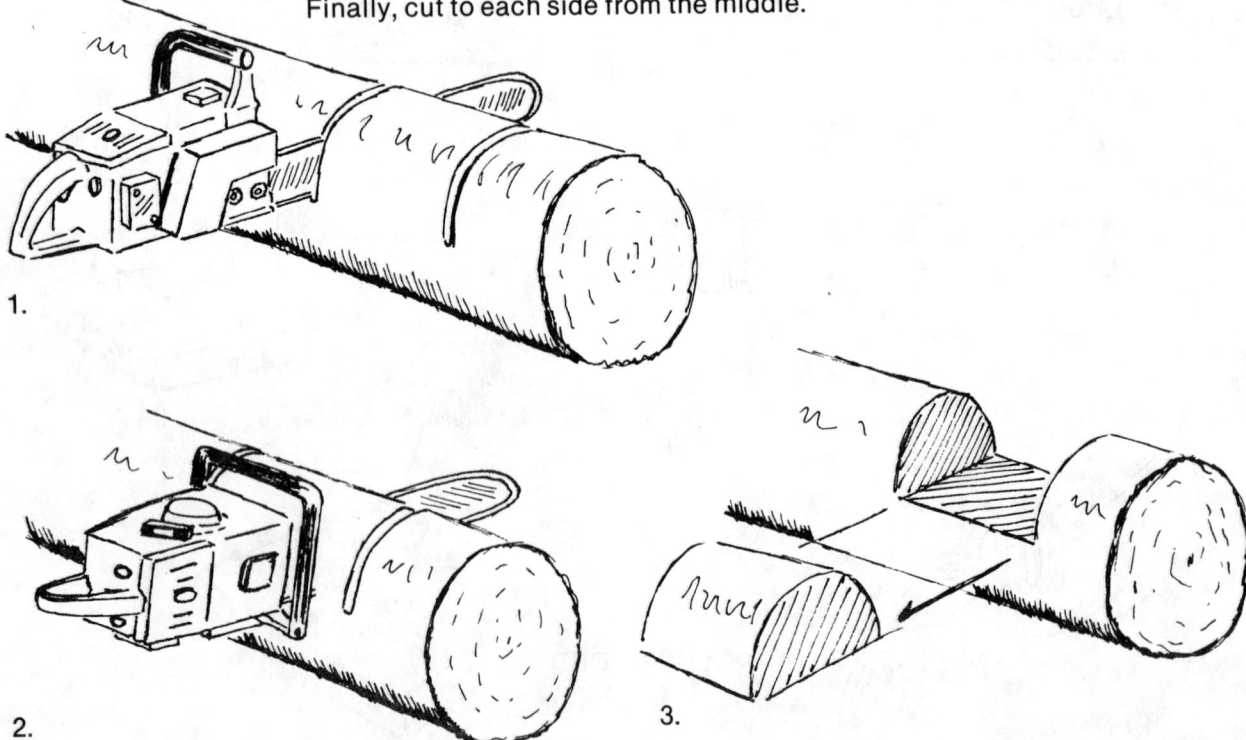

Alternate Method

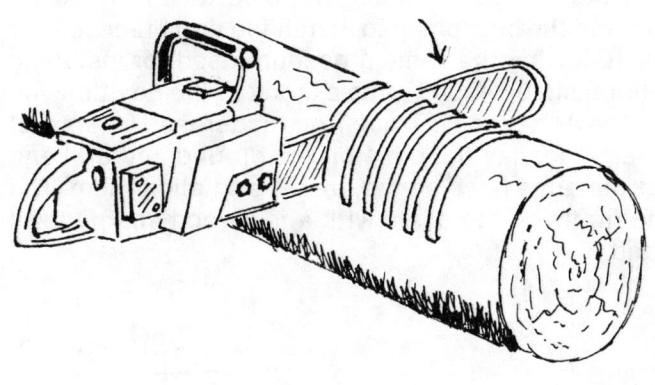

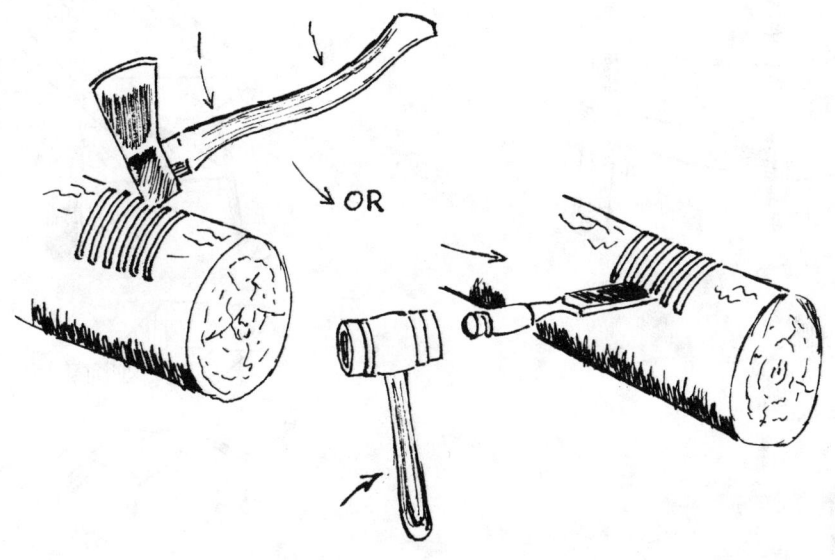

PLANE

Lining Up Inserts

To build projects which require that different sized pieces be inserted at both ends, such as the chair and end table illustrated here, first trace the outline of the smaller piece on the larger piece. For example, trace the inside line of the arms of the horseshoe chair on the surface of the seat. This will make it easier to find the best place to install the arm braces.

Install the arm braces, following the same procedure used for installing table legs. Now set the horseshoe-shaped arms exactly in the position you want them to occupy on the arm braces. Trace from underneath the exact shape and size of each leg. Then lay the arms on the ground and drill and chisel out the holes. Set the arms back on the braces and align them. The arms can then be seated firmly on the posts with a few good sharp blows from the palm of your hand.

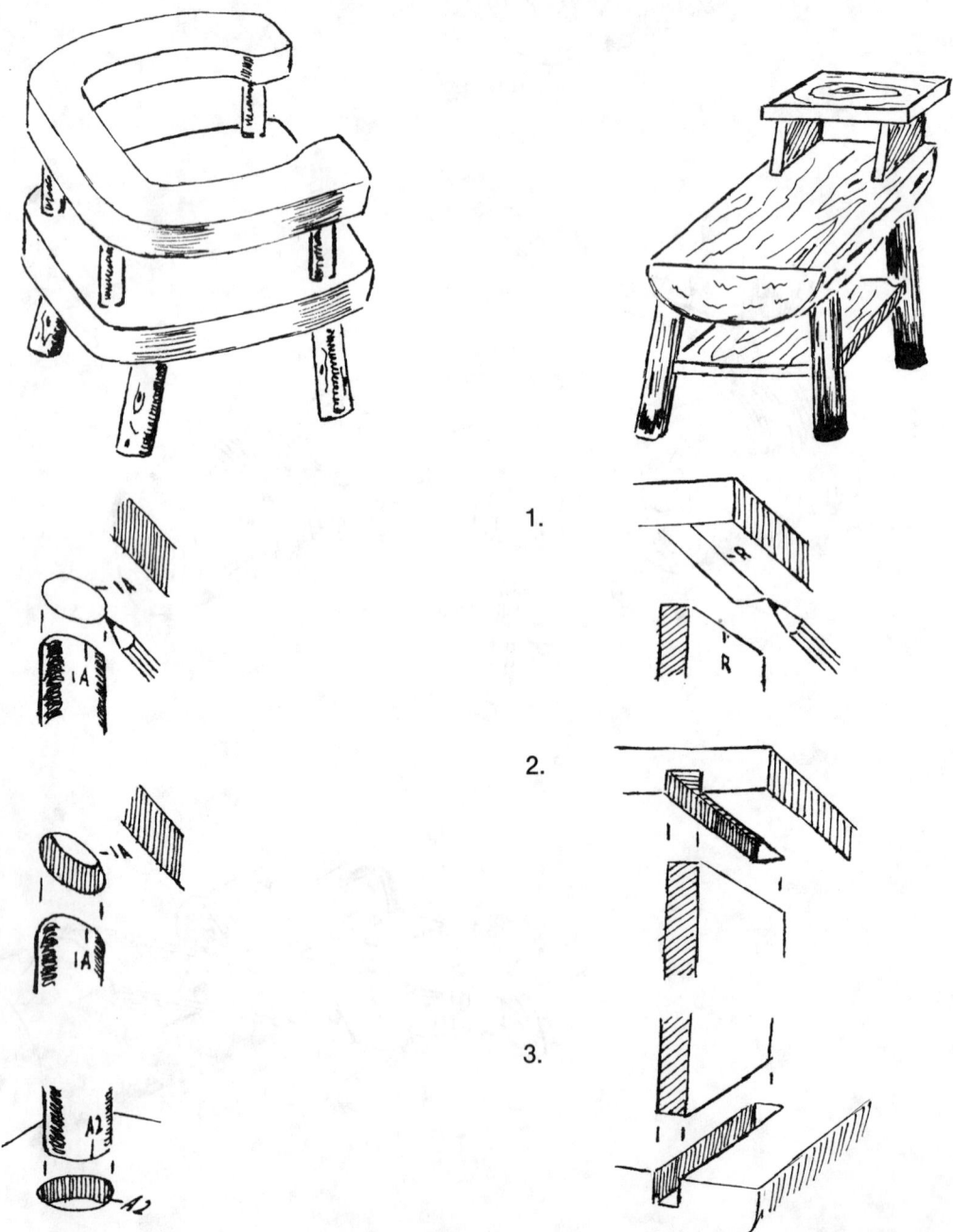

More Examples

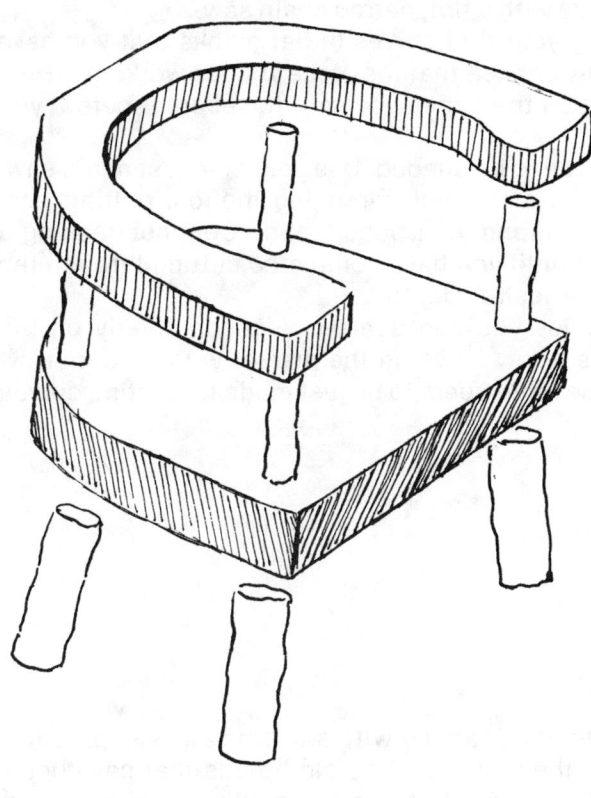
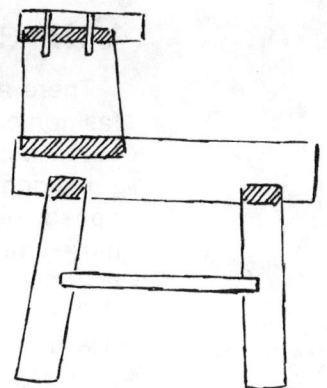
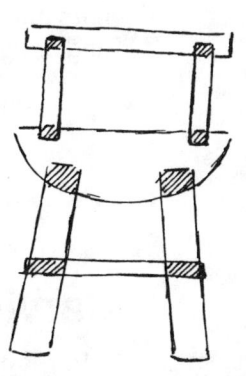

Curves

There are literally thousands of useful and artistic items that you can fashion once you master cutting curves with your chain saw. The trick is to obtain a curved line or surface with a flat, barred chain saw.

I suggest you start cutting your first curves in flat planks that you have ripped yourself. If there is any chance that the piece you are working on will move while you are working on the curves, be sure to secure it before you start cutting.

Draw the design on the piece to be shaped. Use your smallest chain saw. Use just the tip of the bar in a rhythmic dragging motion, cutting one-quarter to one-half inch deep along your pencil mark. Continue making a series of cuts in this fashion until you have completed cutting through the piece or you have reached the desired depth.

The sharpness of the curves you can achieve depends chiefly on the width of your bar. There are a few saws on the market with quite narrow bars and almost pointed noses that seem to be just made for cutting curves and carving.

Carving Panels

Perhaps the easiest way to start carving with a chain saw is to practice scribing, routing or inletting the alphabet. Use old boards that have been nailed down at both ends. If you want to see how small you can write the alphabet, start by carving five or six S's, because it has the smallest, sharpest curves of any letter in the alphabet. The smallest S you can make will be the determining factor of how small the rest of your letters will be. The numerals 3 and 8 will be the most sharply curved numbers you can carve for practice. Practice carving a few signs before you start carving pictures. You will be amazed at how easy it is.

To practice carving or engraving pictures on a flat surface, join together a number of old boards or planks of the same thickness with nails and framing to form a working surface of about three feet by four feet. Plan to work large and fill the entire panel with the main subject of your work. In choosing a subject to carve, try to avoid sharp curves. If you choose to carve a large bull elk for instance, chances are you can carve the entire elk and background with your chain saw with the exception of the eyes and nostrils. These must be done with conventional wood carving tools.

Whatever subject you choose to carve, first draw it out three or four times on paper. Try to eliminate the sharp curves by making the curves less sharp or by changing them into points which you can carve with two separate cuts or strokes with your chain saw, rather than one continuous flowing motion. Next, draw your subject onto your practice panel with a crayon or some other easy-to-see marker.

Once you start carving, your marks will soon be covered with sawdust. Your can either blow off the sawdust with your muffler or stop your saw and brush off the sawdust with an old broom.

After you have carved a few practice panels that you are satisfied with, you are ready to start carving on one of your pieces of choice slab board or a panel made of planks, glue, framing, and wood screws.

Outline cut through panel and mounted on velveteen background.

Carving Block Forms

When choosing a subject to carve out of a block of wood, keep in mind the size of your smallest chain saw, the size of the smallest hole you can bore with it, and the sharpest curve you can make.

Another consideration you might wish to keep in mind is the texture you can achieve. Long, thick hair, such as that of most bears and shaggy haired dogs, is not a difficult texture to achieve with a chain saw. The smoother, soft lines of children and young women are quite hard to achieve with a chain saw. Older men and women with lots of character in their faces are more easily carved. Scraggly beards such as mine, have a texture not too difficult to achieve with a chain saw. The textures of birds of prey are simpler to achieve than are the soft, smooth, rounded lines of more delicate-looking, smaller birds. The texture of the heavy neck hair on stag caribou, bull elk and bison, are easily interpreted with a chain saw, as are the coats of coyote, fox, badger, wolverine, wolf, prime bobcat and lynx, raccoon, rabbits, and many other hairy critters.

After choosing a subject to be carved, make several drawings of the subject, one from each side, front, back, top. Then mark out those areas on each of the drawings which can be sawed off in large chunks. Next mark off the areas on the drawing that can be cut off in moderately large chunks.

For practice in chain saw carving, you can use a block of soap or soft wood, carving with a small knife. When carving your subject for practice in soap or wood, keep in mind what you can and cannot do with a chain saw. Carve the practice block as you think you would with a chain saw. First cutting off the largest chunks, then the moderately sized chunks, small chunks, and detailed routing and planing.

The more practice and forethought you put into your carving, the less difficulty you will have achieving a fine chain saw carved subject.

Sample Carving Projects

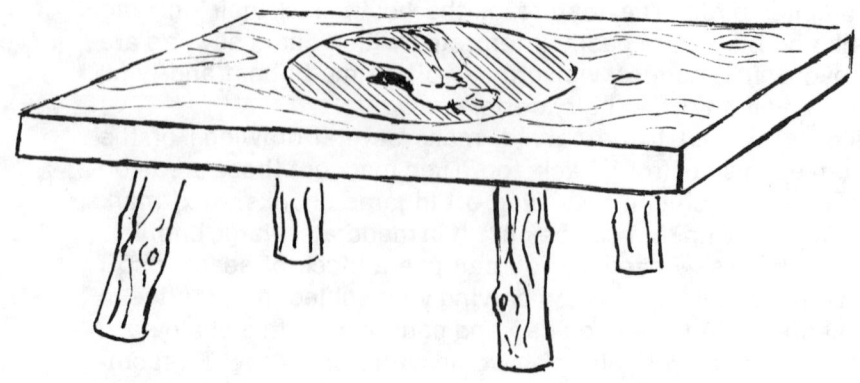

Block Form Projects

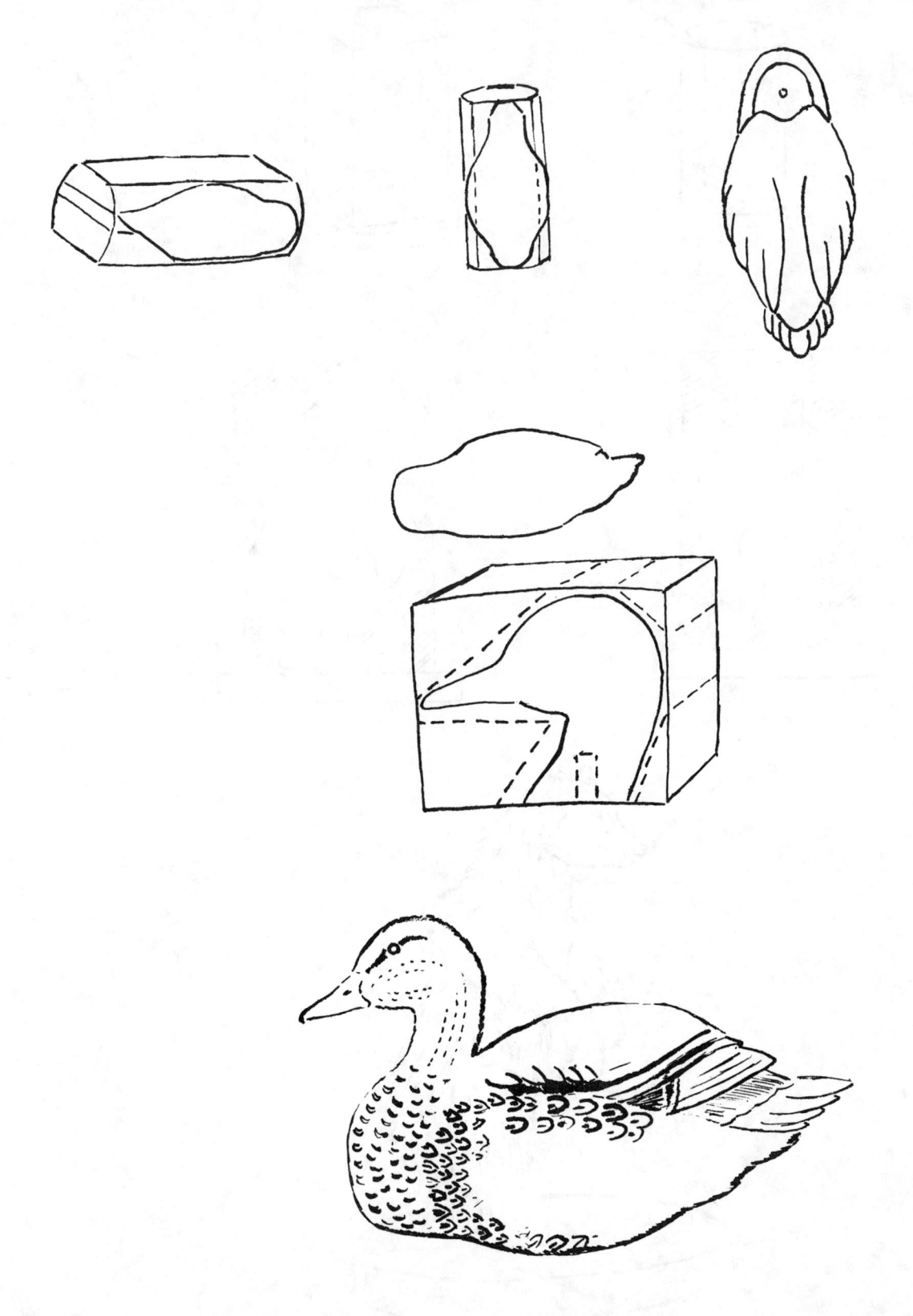

31

More Block Form Projects

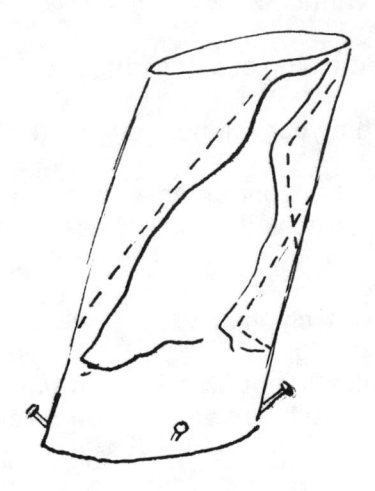

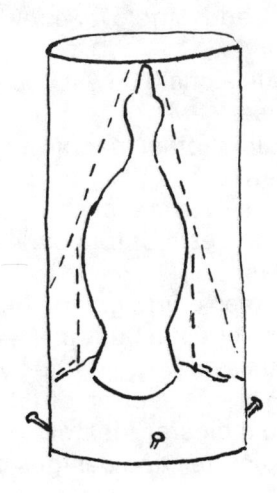

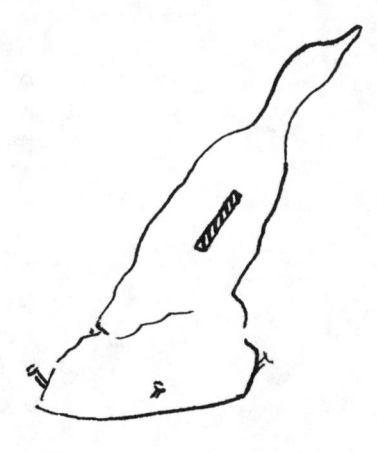

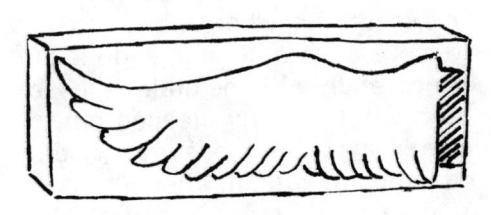

Wing detail

As carving is one of the most dangerous activities you can undertake with a chain saw, and probably thought to be the least dangerous by many people, I will add or go over a few safety precautions.

1. Never run a chain saw if you have been drinking or using drugs, legal or otherwise.
2. Never allow other people to come within your falling distance (or fifteen feet).
3. Always use your least powerful, smallest saw for routing with the tip.
4. Never lose respect for your saw's ability to do you in, regardless of how small it is.
5. Always keep a firm grip on both handles.
6. Never over trust a built-in safety device on a chain saw.
7. Never run a chain saw when you are over fatigued.
8. In the Projects section of this book, I will attempt, with illustrations, to give you a clearer idea of how to achieve both carved block forms and carved pictures and designs on panels.

Hollowing

The following pages on hollowing will attempt to cover most of the types of hollowing necessary to accomplish the projects elsewhere in the book.

Small area hollowing, such as used to make a water dipper, is done by first cutting down in the bowl of the dipper carefully with the grain. If these cuts are close enough together, your bowl will be nearly cleaned out in minutes. If the bowl is not cleaned sufficiently, make another series of cuts inside the bowl perpendicular to the first series of cuts. If, after you have completed both of these series of cuts, the bowl is still not sufficiently clear of wood, carefully keep repeating these series of cuts until you can fan the tip of your bar back and forth to grind out and smooth the inside of the dipper bowl.

Large area hollowing (such as the canoe shown here) is accomplished first by drawing the inside line of the piece to be worked. Using the tip of your bar, scribe the line deeply into the wood so you can see it easily when the chips start flying. Now compare the length of your bar with the desired greatest depth you will be cutting. If the bar is longer than that depth, you may want to mark it with paint or ink so you will not penetrate the piece too deeply. Next cut the desired depth outlining the hollow. Now, cutting with the grain, first cut your bar into the piece, then rip with the grain. Remove the largest pieces possible. Repeat this process, as shown in the canoe drawing, until the hollowing is nearly completed. The remainder of the unwanted wood in the bottom of the piece can be removed in the same manner used in small area hollowing described previously.

Through hollowing is easiest to achieve when you can find a piece that is already hollow, partially hollow, or soft and pulpy on the inside and hard and sound on the outside.

The drawing for through hollowing shows a series of plunge cuts made in one direction then other cuts made perpendicular to them. The waste is then knocked out. The remainder of the hollowing is done by cutting on an oblique angle to the other cuts. To complete the hollowing, grind and plane smooth the inside by gliding your saw over the rough interior of the piece with your saw idling slowly.

Small Area Hollowing

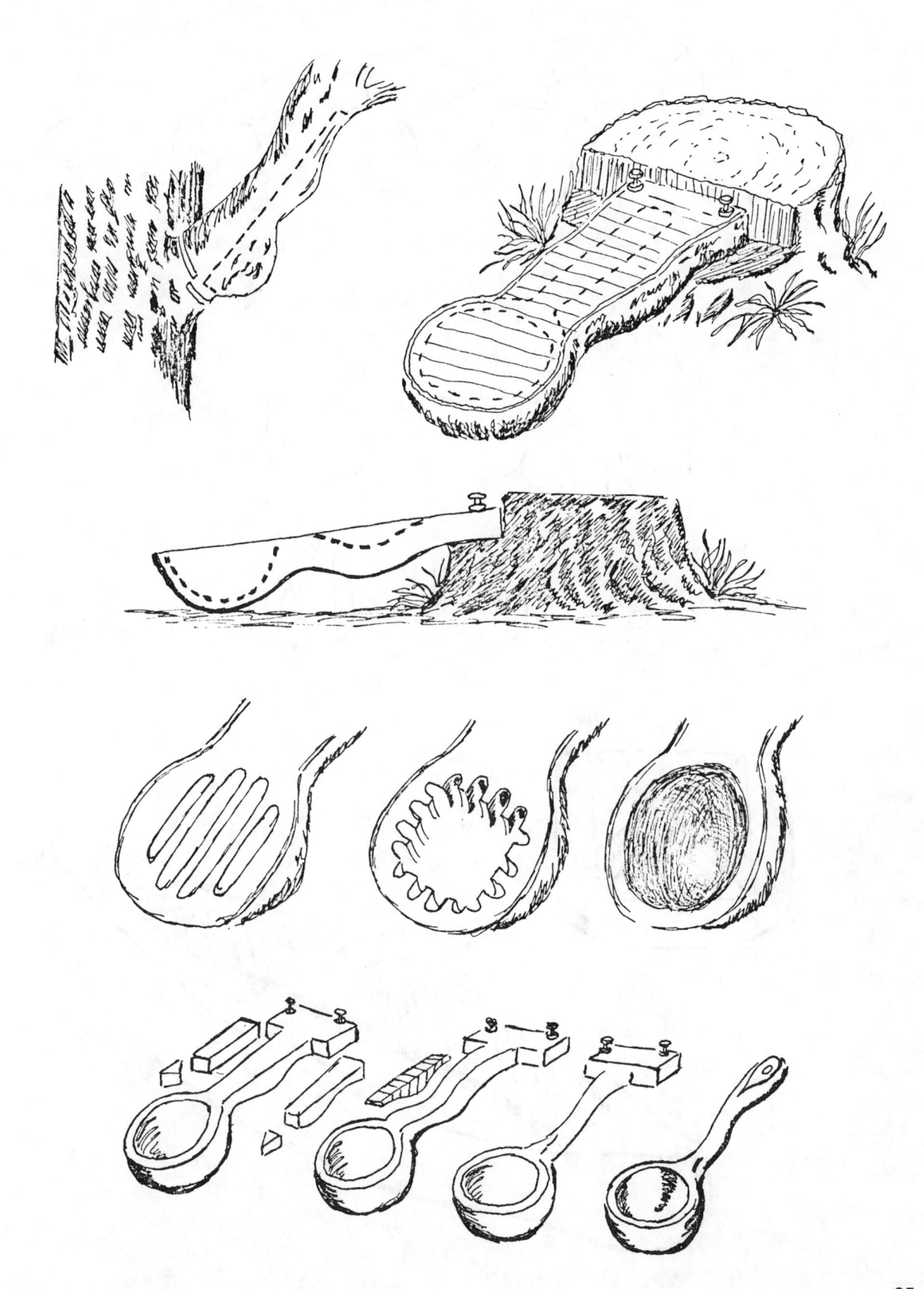

35

Large Area Hollowing

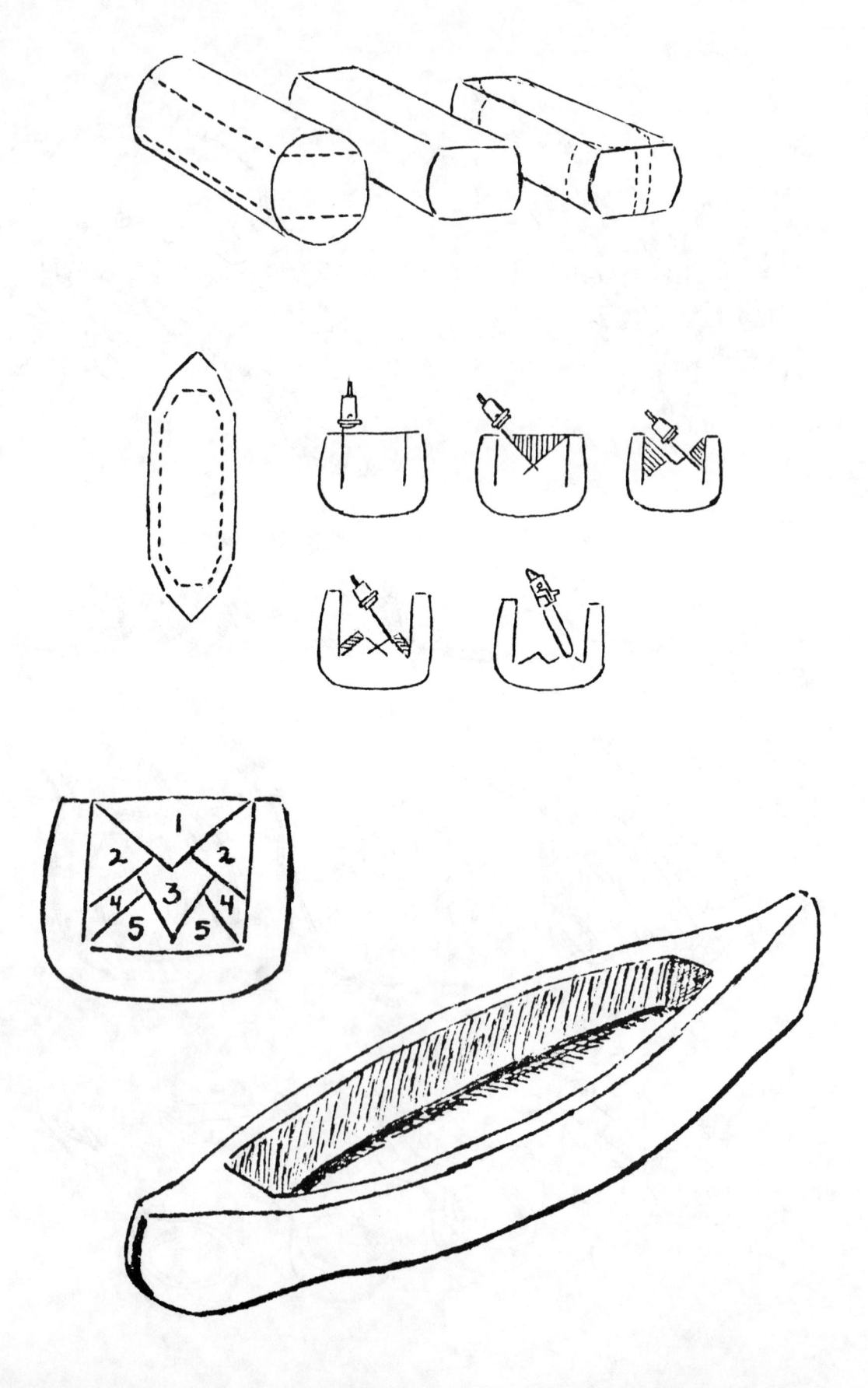

Through Hollowing

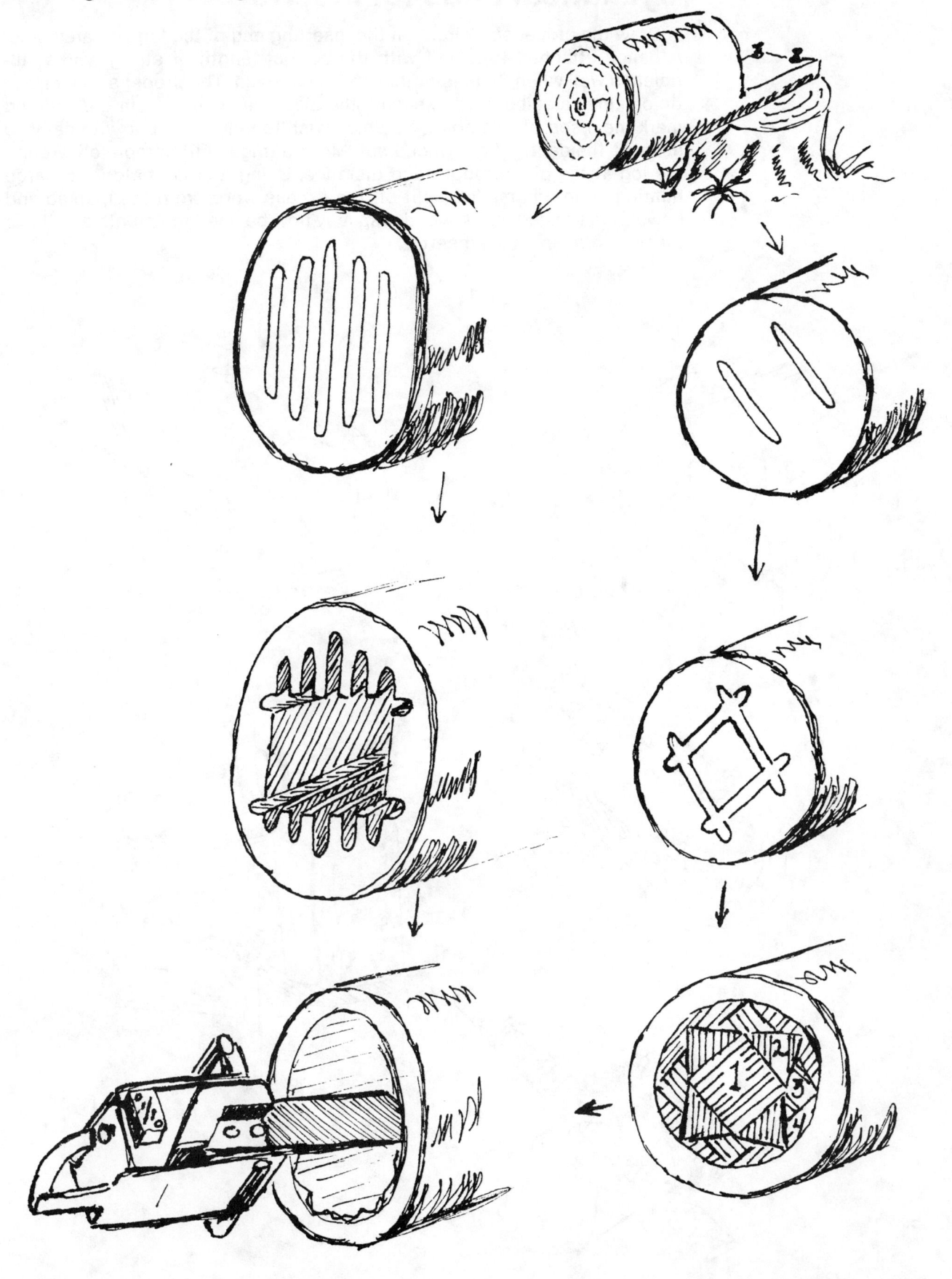

Cylindrical Ends for Inserts

Draw the proper size circle on the inserting end of the log you are using. A pencil attached to a nail with the correct length of string works sufficiently well when there is nothing better at hand. The proper size jar lid or tin can may also be used. Measure the distance desired from the end and mark the insert at this point. You may wish to mark your bar with paint to indicate the depth of the ringed cut. Make a ringed cut completely around the log at the proper depth and distance. Using a small hatchet or large hunting knife and mallet, split off the excess wood from the marked end down to the ringed cut. A wood rasp may now be used to smooth any flaws that may remain on the insert.

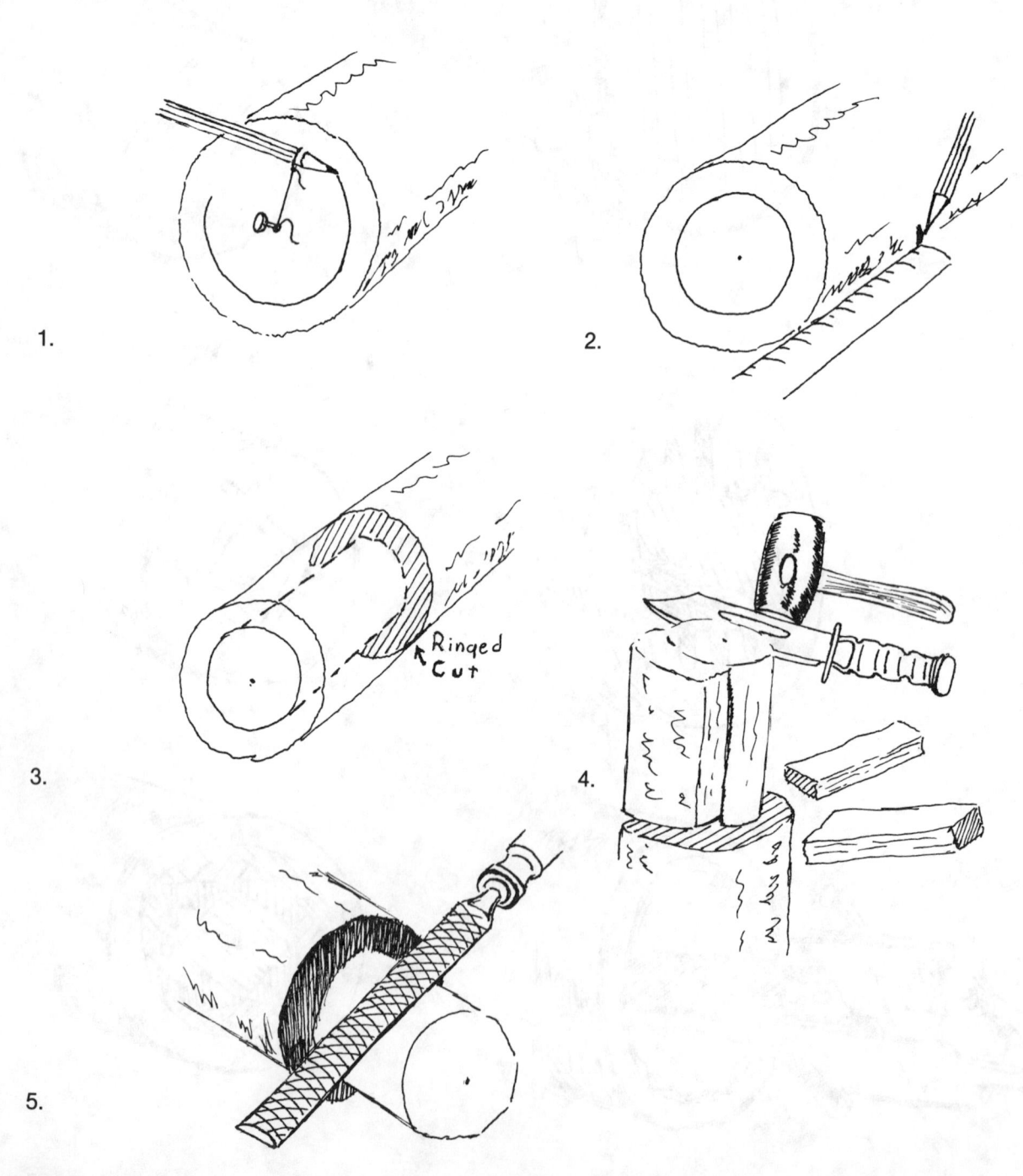

1.

2.

3.

4.

5.

Squaring Ends for Inserts

Measure and draw a square on the end of the log. Measure and mark the length to be squared. Make four right angle cuts, just touching at their shallowest point. Drawings four through seven show slabbing off the four sides following the drawn lines to form a square on the end of the log and the four right angle cuts at the rear. I prefer to roll the log to the right after each cut so I am working off the left side and away from the piece. You may wish to clean up any imperfections with a wood rasp.

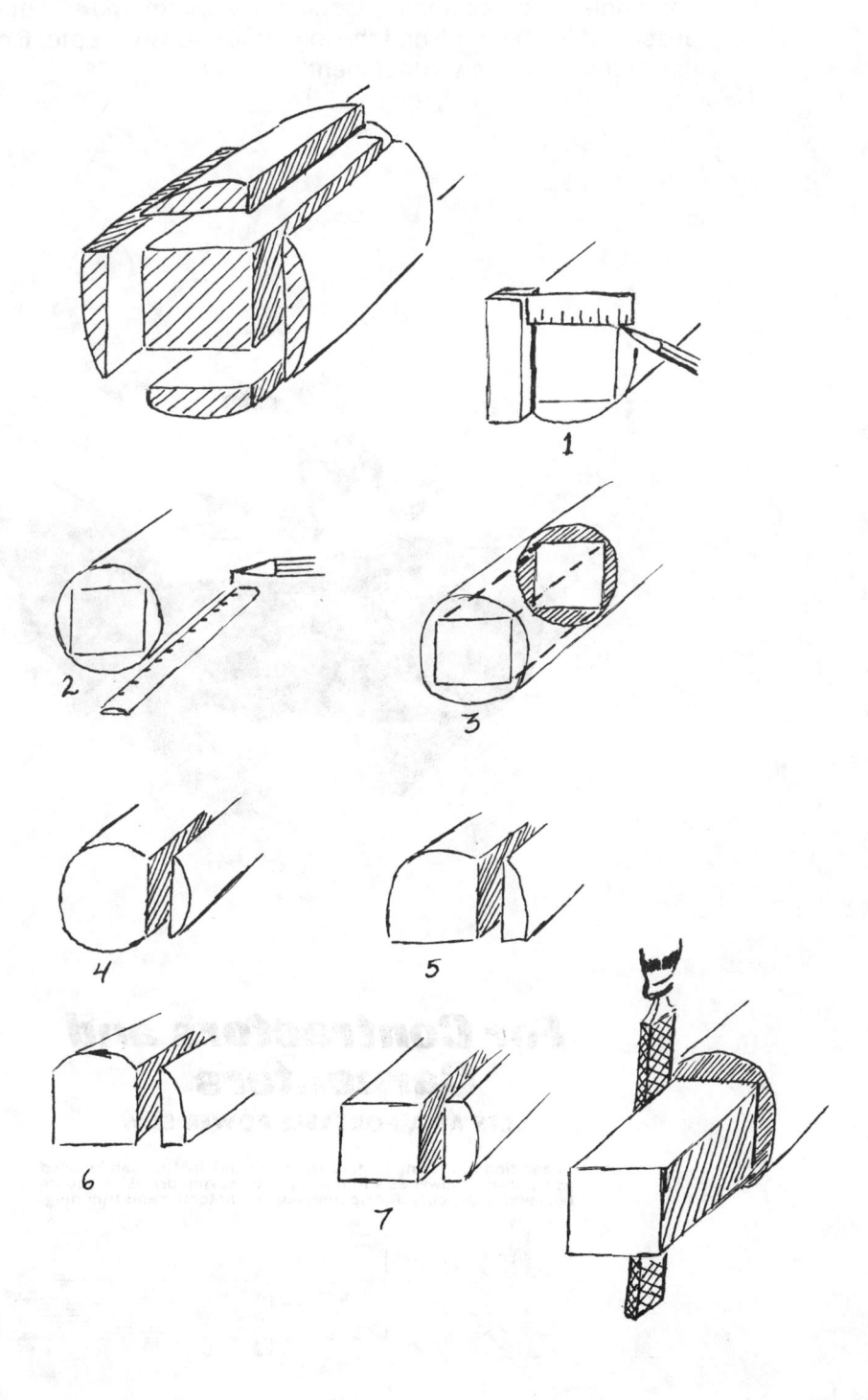

Mini Mill

The Mini Mill attachment shown on these two pages can be combined with your chain saw to convert the two tools into a single precision lumber-making mill. The Mini Mill quickly makes smooth ready-to-use dimensioned lumber into logs of any thickness. Boards of any size can then be made from the logs.

The Mini Mill can also be used as a portable power saw to make square and angle cuts, for ripping, edging, notching, and trimming. The projects described in chapter 5 and the log structures in chapter 6 could make good use of this chain saw attachment.

For Contractors and Carpenters
ACTS AS A PORTABLE POWER SAW

In addition to making lumber from logs, MINI-MILL can be used as a portable power saw in making time-saving precision square cuts and angle cuts, for ripping, edging, notching and trimming.

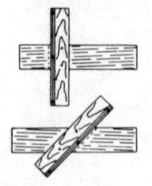

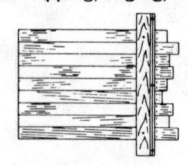

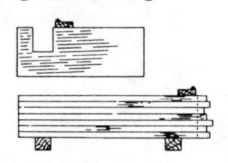

THIS IS HOW IT WORKS

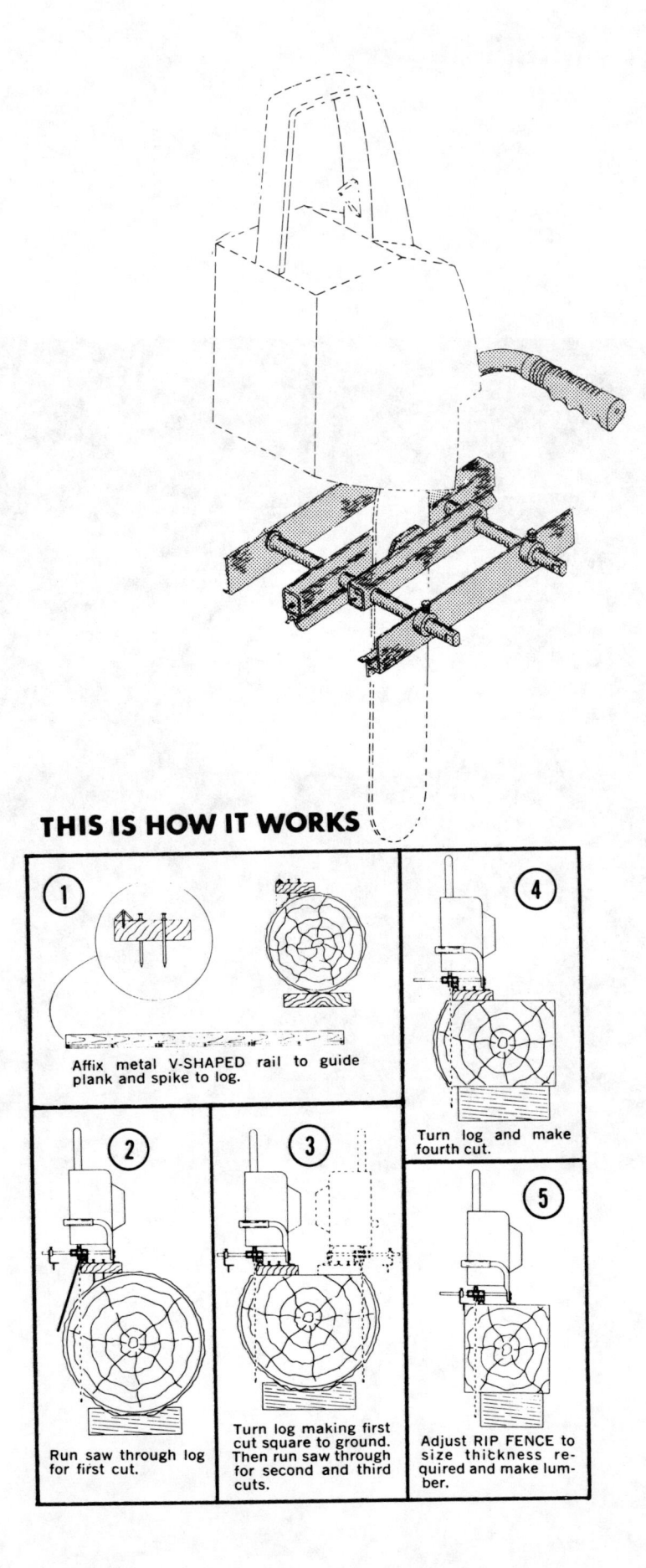

1. Affix metal V-SHAPED rail to guide plank and spike to log.

2. Run saw through log for first cut.

3. Turn log making first cut square to ground. Then run saw through for second and third cuts.

4. Turn log and make fourth cut.

5. Adjust RIP FENCE to size thickness required and make lumber.

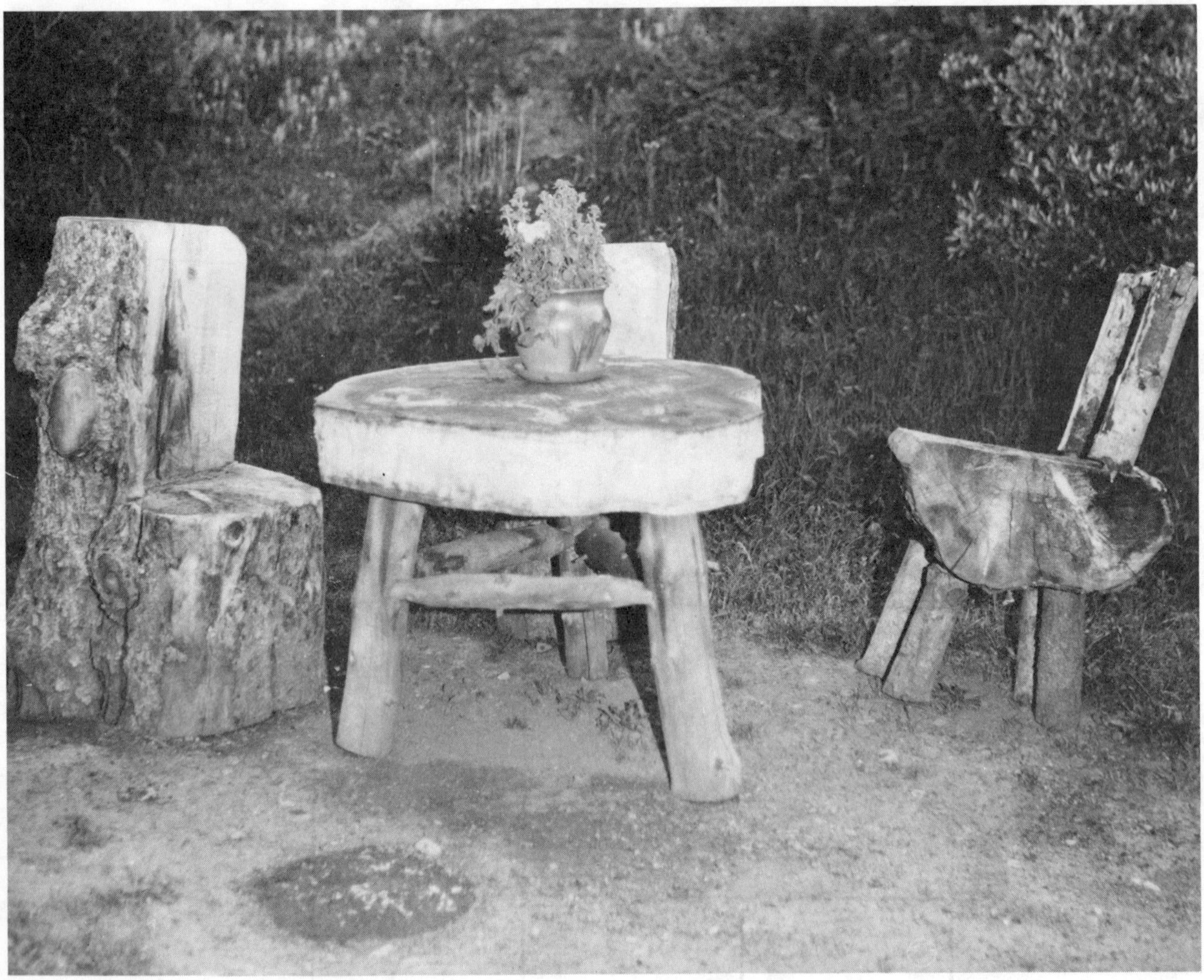

5. Projects

Now that you have become somewhat familiar with the basic techniques of handling your chain saw, we can proceed with the actual construction of the many and varied projects which can be made with a chain saw.

Chairs

Chair One

This chair is a good starting place for the beginner. I suggest that you make five or six of these chairs before going on to more involved projects.

The best looking chairs of this type are made from the base of a tree or from tree stumps. However, any piece of log large enough will work fine.

I find the easiest and most comfortable way for me to carve this chair with the least amount of strain on the saw, is to lay the log on top of several supporting logs, so as to keep the bar and chain out of the dirt.

First, make the cut for the back of the chair by cutting straight down from the end of the log, being careful not to cut too deeply into the supports. Then, roll the log until the cut you have made is parallel with the ground. Now make the vertical cut for the seat, perpendicular to the ground, but do not pass the first cut. If cuts do not meet evenly, make the necessary corrections.

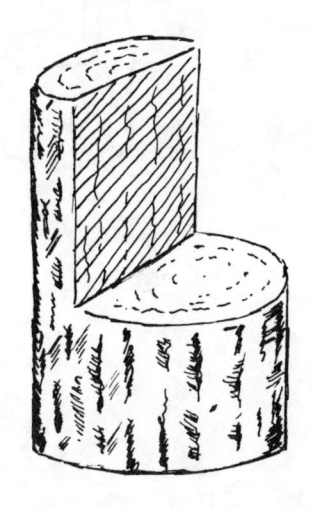

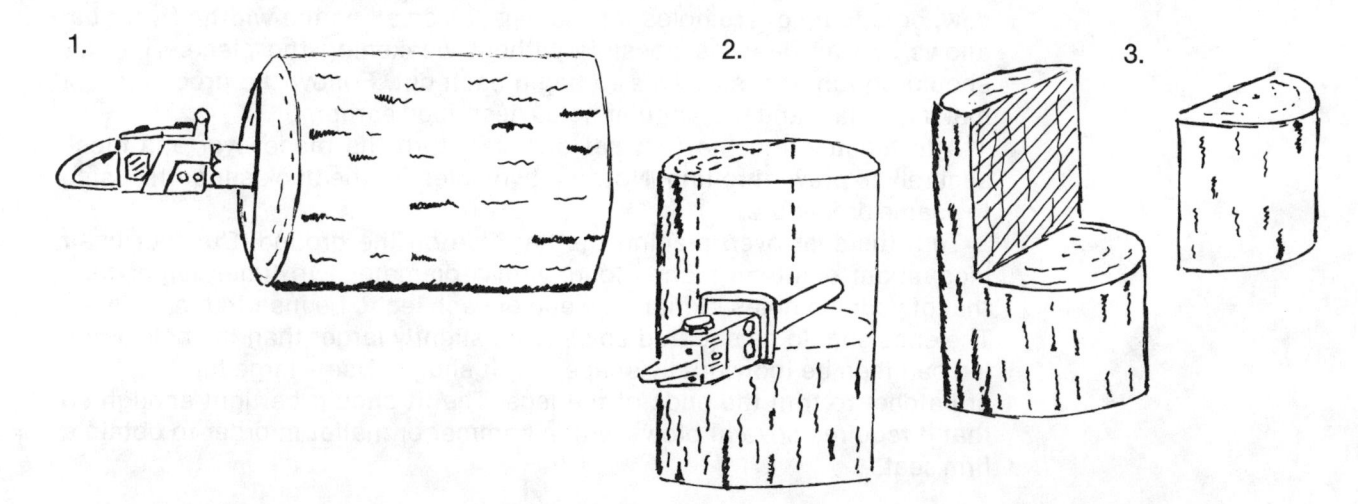

Chair Two

This chair is begun in the same way as number one; it can then be made somewhat more elaborate and comfortable by cutting out a wedge in the back as shown in the illustration.

After the wedge has been removed, the back can be rounded out to fit the contour of your body by simply holding the saw firmly, running at a slow idle use the tip of the bar. This last step will also provide good practice for more involved projects later on.

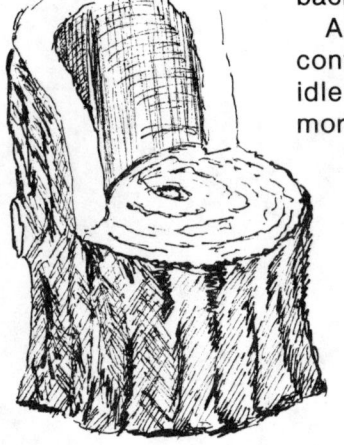

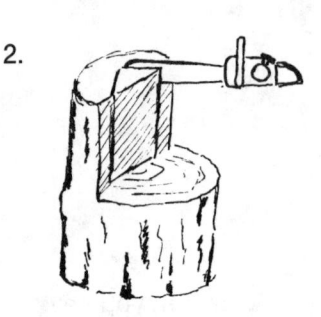

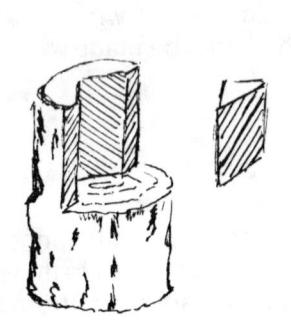

Chair Three

This chair can often be made with pieces left over from the first two chairs.

Place the half round piece flat on the ground. Using your narrowest chain saw, bore four square holes for the legs, as small as the width of your bar allows and as deep as possible without weakening the piece. The saw should be run at a slow idle to begin each cut. Follow the procedure for making square and rectangular holes described earlier.

After completing the first set of holes, turn the piece over and block securely to prevent rolling. Now cut two holes for the back supports, using the same procedure.

Turn the seat over, placing the flat side on the ground. Cut four chair legs, about eighteen inches long, with a diameter two times larger than that of your leg holes. Square the end of each leg to be inserted in the hole. The ends should be squared so as to be slightly larger than the hole. Each leg can then be individually shaped to fit snugly. Use a large hunting knife or hatchet to trim the ends of the legs. The fit should be tight enough so that it requires several blows with a hammer or mallet in order to obtain a firm seat.

After the legs are firmly seated and the chair turned right side up, the four legs will probably be uneven. To correct this, first make certain the chair is on a level spot. Then mark each leg, so that when cut, all four will be of equal length.

After the legs have been evened off, again stand the chair right side up and carve the two upright back pieces in the same manner as the legs. As with the legs, these uprights should then be seated firmly with a mallet or hammer.

To make the slots in the uprights, make three cuts approximately two to four inches deep, almost touching each other. Run the saw slowly to begin each cut. These slots will require little or no cleaning.

To finish the back piece, lay it on top of the uprights and mark the position and width of the slots. Now lay the marked back piece on the ground and cut the desired notches by making a series of shallow cuts in the marked area. The notches may be smoothed by gliding the chain saw at an idle, sideways over the notch. Periodically check the fit by testing it in the notches of the uprights. The fit should be firm, but not so tight that the upright will be split when the back piece is seated.

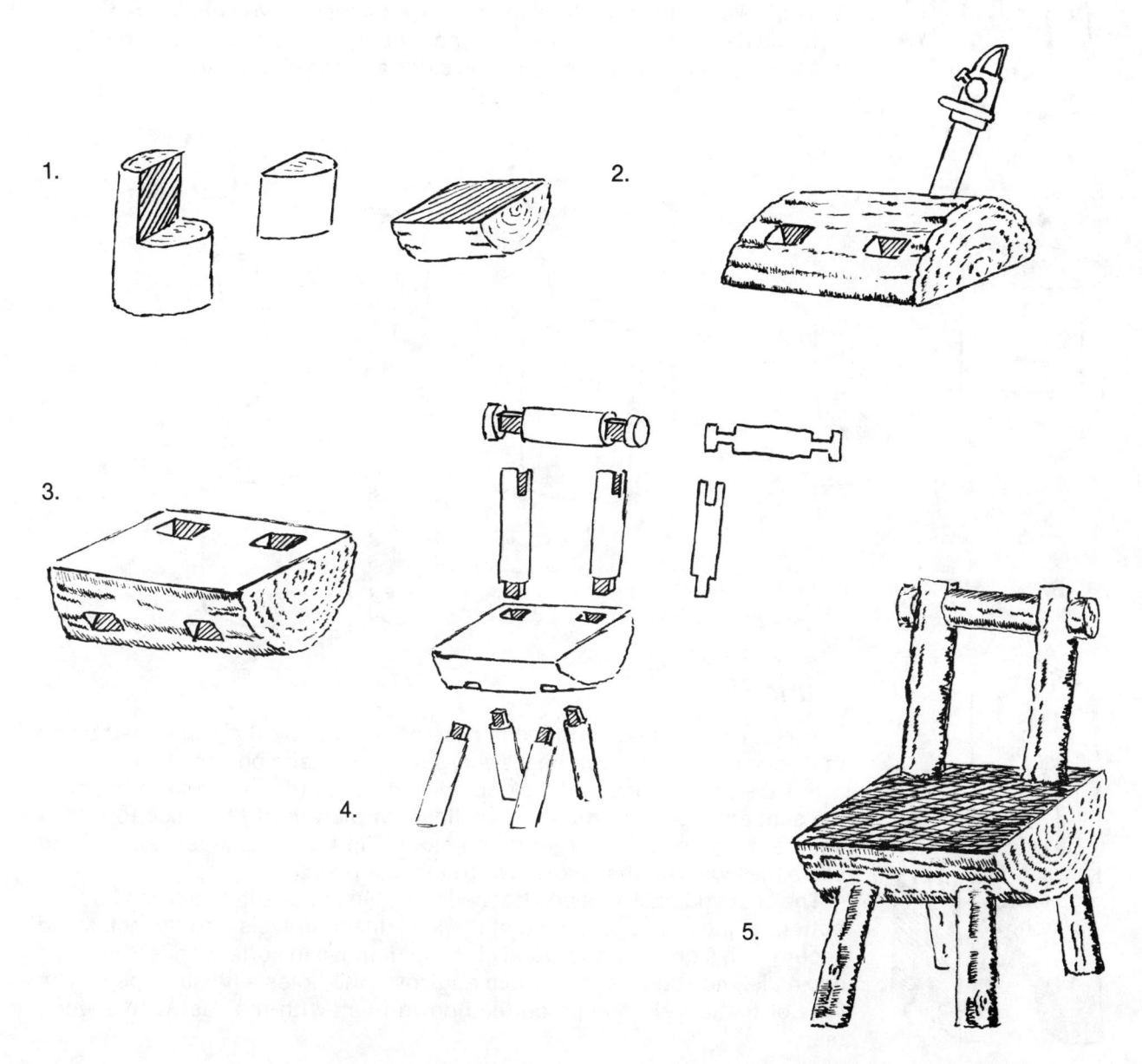

1.

2.

3.

4.

5.

45

Chair Four

Both the back and seat are made in the same way as chairs one and two; however a shorter block must be used because legs will be added later in a separate operation.

After the back and seat have been cut out, turn the chair upside down and brace it on the block you have just removed. There are several ways to bore the leg holes. One method is with a brace and bit or an electric drill: make numerous holes in a circle, then remove the excess wood with a mallet and gouge. You can also make these holes in the same way as with chair three, using your smallest chain saw. However, if you do use a chain saw, it will be necessary to use larger legs since you will not be able to cut out holes as small as with a drill.

The easiest method I have found for making the notched part of the chair leg is to first measure the depth of each hole. Mark this depth on the leg, then carry the mark all of the way around the leg with a saw. Using a hatchet or hunting knife, split the wood down to the ringed cut. After the legs are finished, seat firmly into the holes using a hammer or mallet. If the legs are not level, square them off in the same manner as with chair three.

If you desire a chair with a little more flourish, you can carve a design in the back, just round off or shape the sides and top of the back.

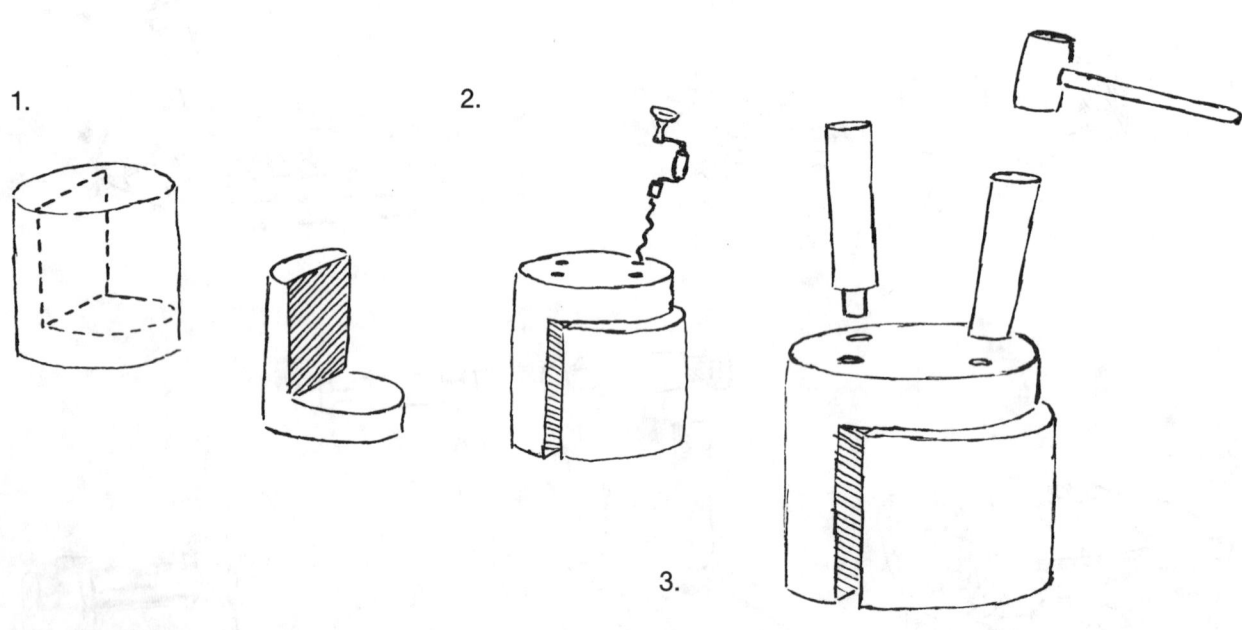

1.

2.

3.

Chair Five

The back and seat of this chair are also made by the same method as that used on number four, and is very similar to chairs one and two.

For the legs, choose a block somewhat larger than the one from which the seat and back are made. Draw lines on the top of the block to form a square, then cut off the four round sides. Tip the block upside down and carve the legs with the chain saw to suit your taste.

The seat and back can be attached by drilling one-half inch holes into the bottom of the seat and the top of the legs. Insert dowels into the holes and secure with a good strong wood glue. Sometimes in softer conifers you can use nails, then counter-sink them and cover the holes with short pegs. The tops of the dowels should be filed down flush with the seat with a wood rasp.

Chair Five—Method

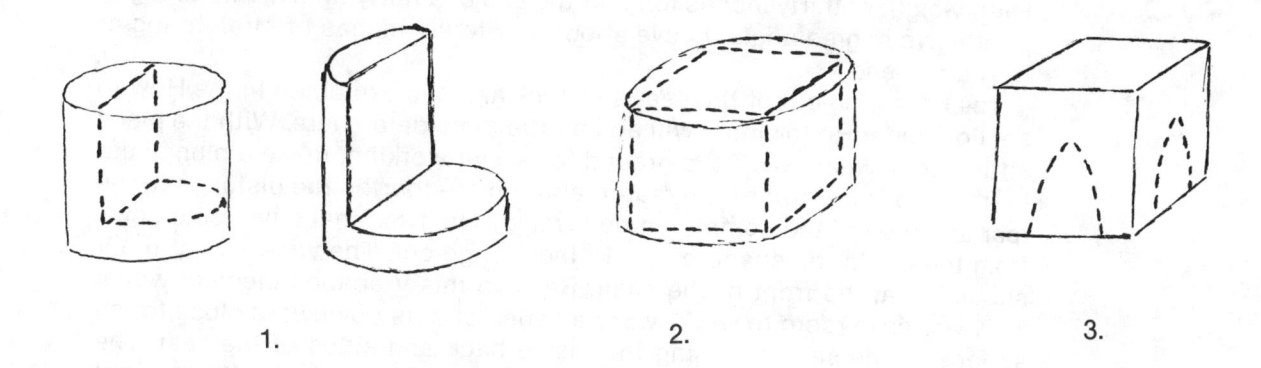

1.
2.
3.

Chair Six

First determine the overall height of the chair and select a block of wood to fit. Draw lines on one end to form a square. The square should not measure less than twenty inches across.

Lay the piece on the ground and, cutting from the marked end, cut off the four round sides. Roll the piece over for each new cut.

Draw on the block exactly where you want the back of the seat and the legs. Position the piece so as to have the leg markings facing up. Now cut and carve out the excess wood between the four legs. Then tip the piece right side up and cut out the seat and back.

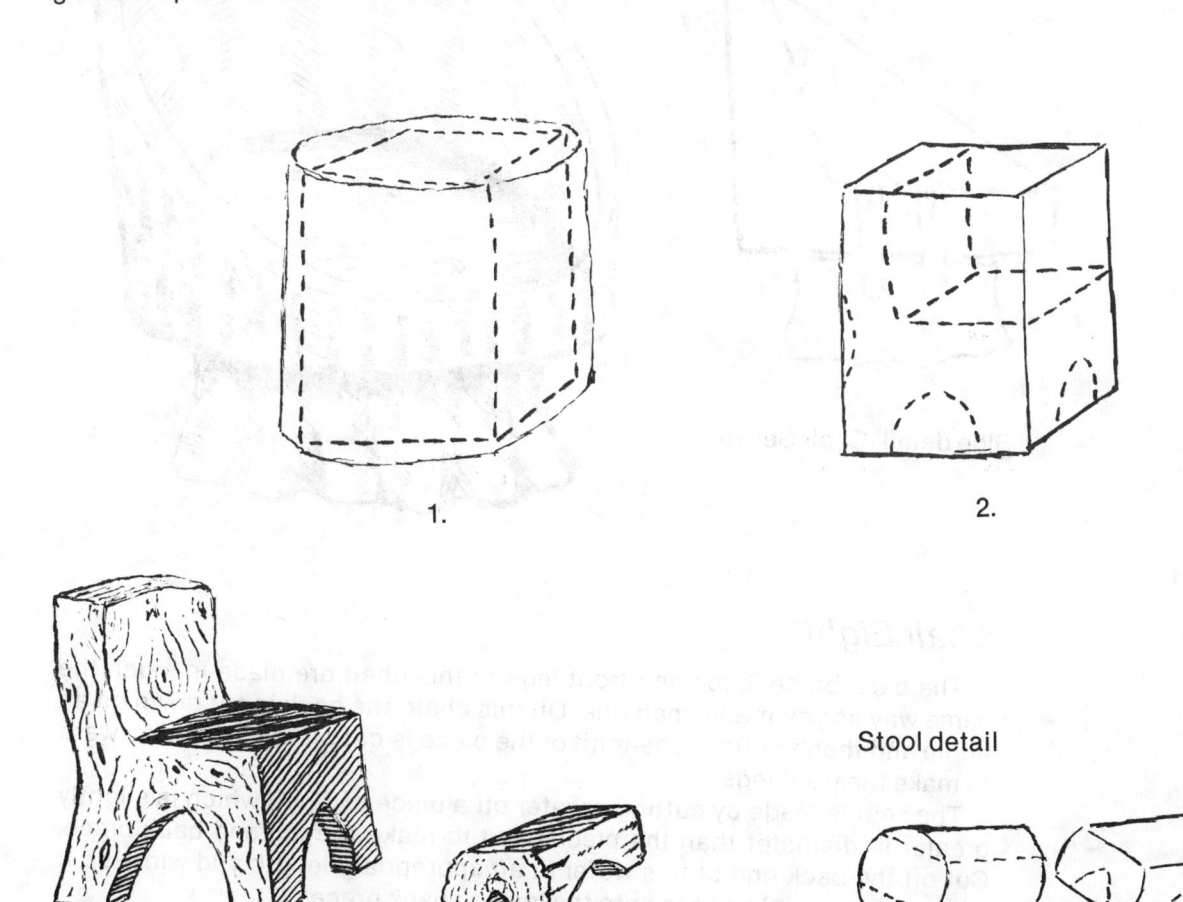

1.
2.

Stool detail

Chair Seven

The seat and back of chair seven are made by cutting a block about twenty-eight or thirty inches long off the end of a thirty inch diameter log at a forty-five degree angle. Leave about four to six inches of straight log at the narrow end.

The hollowing-out of the seat and back areas is explained in the How-to section under Hollowing. I will add a little more detail here. With the piece sitting somewhat up off the ground for easier working, make a plunge cut in from the front toward the rear to about three-fourths the distance to the rear and side of the completed hollowing area. Next make two cuts down from the top in the shape of a V to the plunge cut. The wide end of the V should be at the front of the chair. Remove this V shaped piece of wood. Now you have room to work. Make a series of cuts downward close to the surface of the seat, touching the inside back and sides of the seat. The cuts should be made about one-quarter of an inch apart and will knock out easily with a hammer. Keep a firm grip and a slow idle on your saw as you plane and rout out the remainder of the excess wood. There are hundreds of styles of legs you can use on this chair; however the one illustrated is merely an apple stump with large dowels held in with wooden wedges.

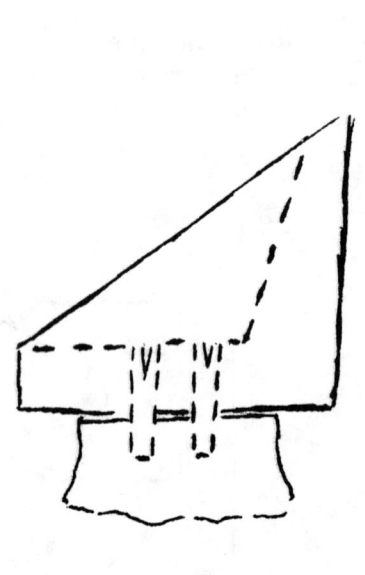

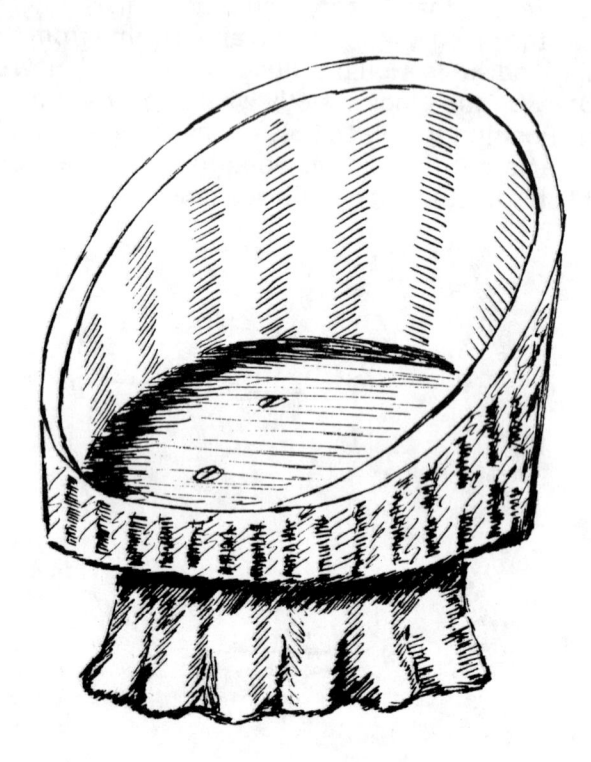

Side detail, Chair Seven

Chair Eight

The back brace, back and front legs of this chair are made in much the same way as you made chair one. On this chair, the back is cut down on an angle and then the front one-third of the piece is cut off and moved forward to make the front legs.

The seat is made by cutting a wafer off a piece of wood which is slightly greater in diameter than the piece used to make the leg and back brace. Cut off the back end of this wafer at an appropriate length and width so it looks proportional and fits onto the leg and back brace.

The backrest of this chair is not as simple as it may appear at first glance. You will need an oval-shaped wafer the same thickness as the seat. To obtain this backrest, use the same log from which you cut the seat wafer. Make both cuts to obtain this wafer on a twenty to thirty degree angle to your previous straight cross cut. Now that you have this long, oval-shaped backrest, measure across the back of the seat wafer. Use this measurement to determine where to cut the backrest across short ways; the bottom of the backrest and the back of the seat should meet evenly.

The method for joining the backrest and the seat may vary. You may wish to angle and join these pieces as shown in the drawings or you may wish to have the seat continue back and form fit the backrest and leg component of this chair, then form fit the backrest to the seat.

This chair looks best when the seat and back extend at least one inch beyond the legs. The chair is now ready to be joined with glue and dowels.

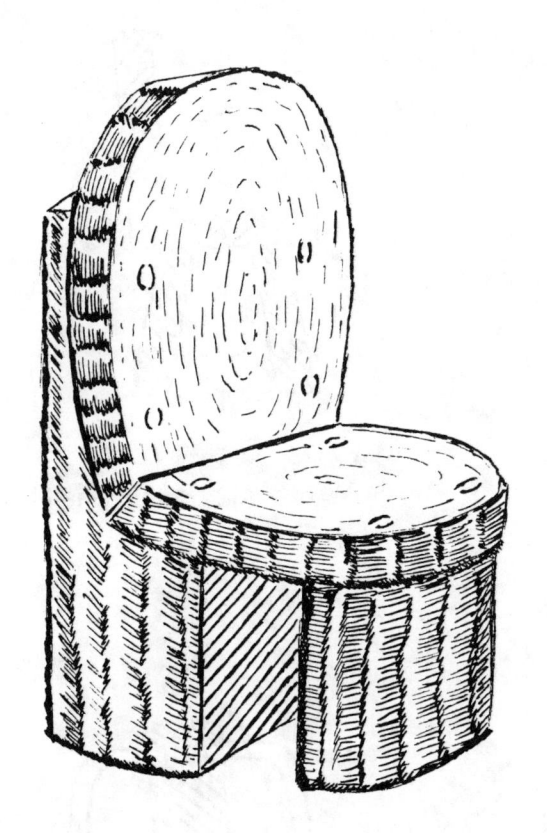

Side detail, Chair Eight

Chairs Nine and Ten

Chairs nine and ten begin in the same way and follow the same basic instructions as chair four. The main difference is a slight difference in the back design. While chair nine has only a slight rounded top on the semi-concave back, chair ten's back is somewhat more involved.

Leaving a strip about ten inches wide for a backrest support, round off the top of the backrest as shown in the drawing for chair ten. There are several ways to achieve the two additional back supports. You may wish to find a limb with a bend or a crook in it about four times the thickness of your desired supports. Begin by ripping off both sides of this limb. Then ripping it down the middle, to make your outer supports. You will have to use a knife or wood rasp to complete fashioning these supports. Of course, the easiest way to achieve the supports is to find two limbs of the correct diameter and bend them for the project. A third way is to use green limbs of the correct diameter, peel and bend them to suit your needs.

When installing these supports, you will have to allow one inch inward on the seat and one inch down on the back brace to accommodate the depth of the two side braces. Draw the outline of these holes, then use a one-quarter inch electric drill around the outline on the inside. Remove the excess with a gouge or chisel and mallet. These outer supports may need to be glued or doweled from the rear.

Chair Nine

Side detail, Chair Nine

Chair Ten

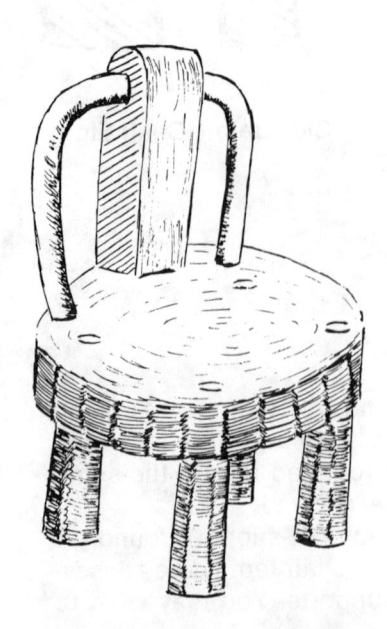

Back detail, Chair Ten

Chair Fourteen (foreground) and Flat Slab Chair in background (see page 55).

Chairs Eleven, Twelve, Thirteen and Fourteen

Chairs eleven, twelve, thirteen and fourteen are basically the same. They each employ the use of a flat slab for the seat and round small logs for the legs, back and arms. Chair fourteen, however, has a shelf under the seat that also acts as a brace, making this chair almost indestructible. This shelf brace is installed from the side of the chair after the other parts are assembled. Use a slab about one inch thick for this shelf. Cut the sides of the shelf about one-half inch narrower than the outer dimension of the legs from one side to the other. Measure the distance from the inside of the front legs to the inside of the back legs. Add about one and one-half inches to this measurement and cut the front and back of the shelf to this length. Now place the shelf against the outside of the legs about halfway between the seat and the floor. Mark with a pencil on a front and back leg where you will want the shelf. Trace the outline of the shelf here. Next notch out these tracings with your chain saw. Do the same thing from the other side. Now slide the shelf in from the side and glue or dowel it into place.

The other skills needed to build these four chairs are explained in detail in the preceding chapter on How-to under Slots and Grooves and Round Holes and Ripping Boards.

Chair Eleven—Method

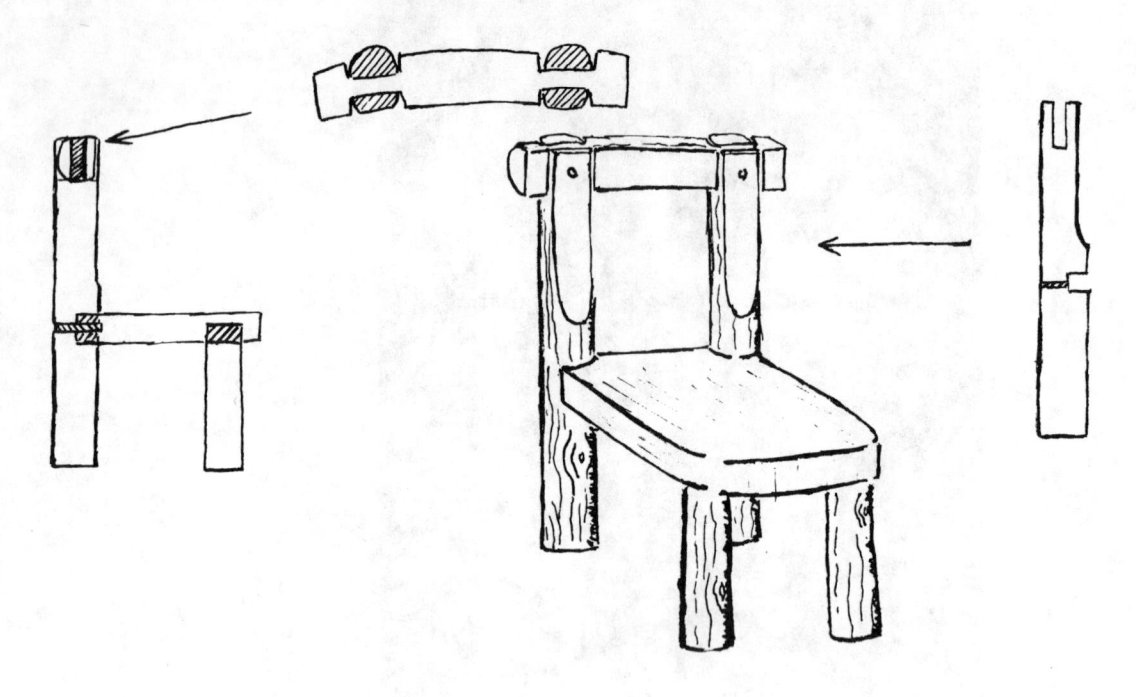

Chair Twelve—Method

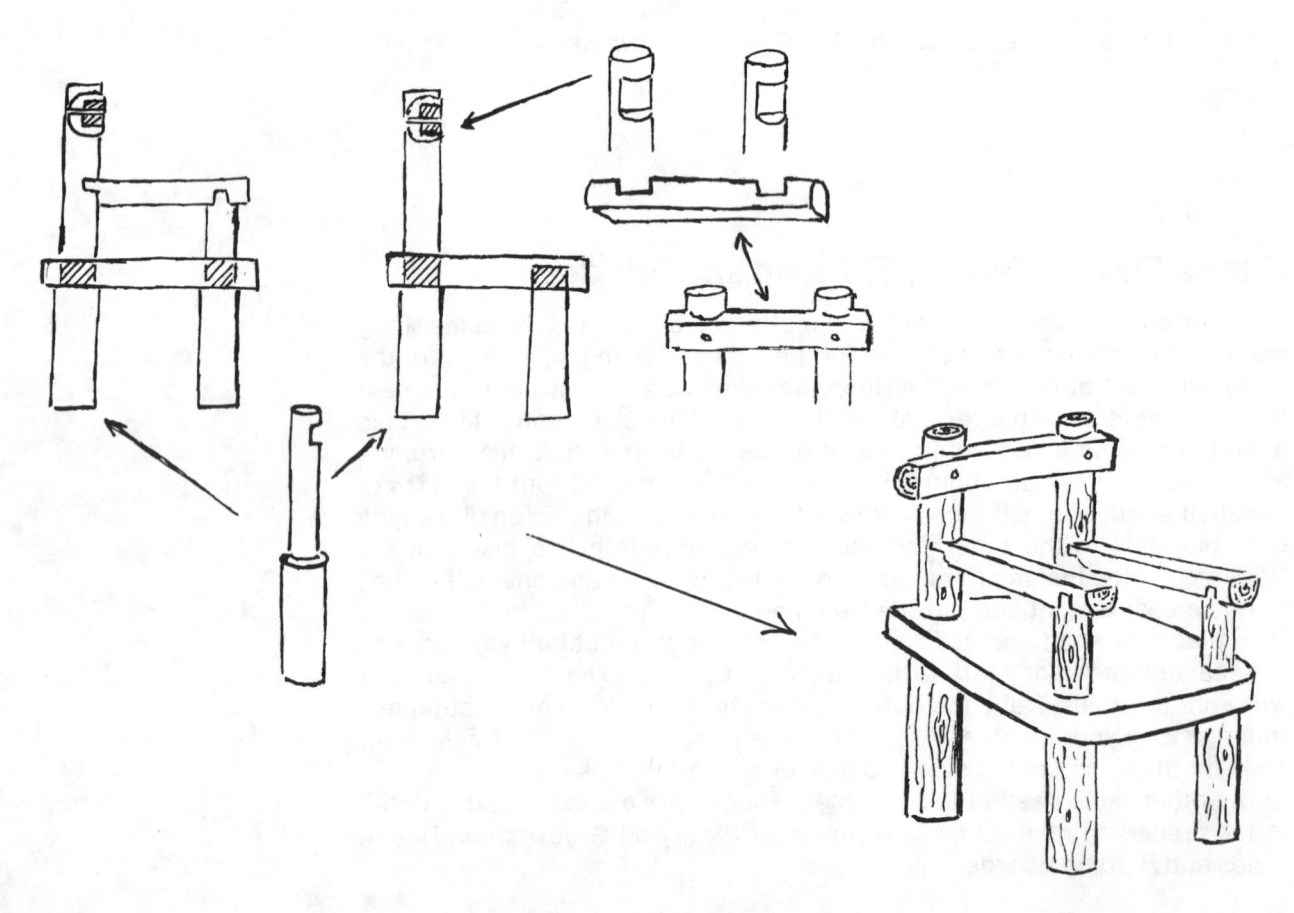

52

Chair Thirteen—Method

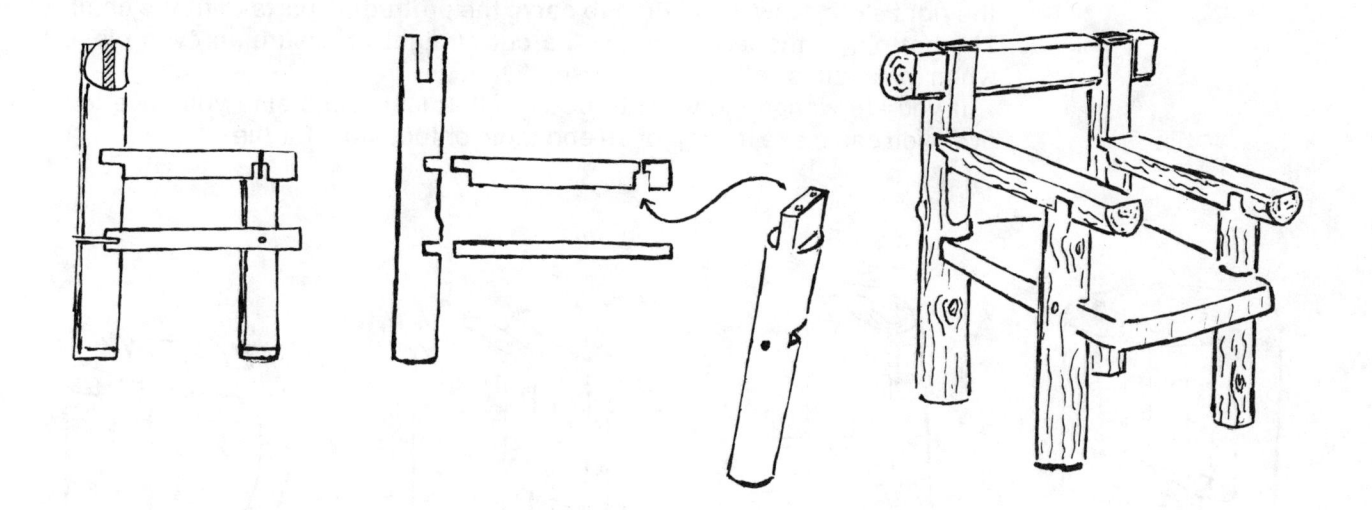

Chair Fourteen—Method

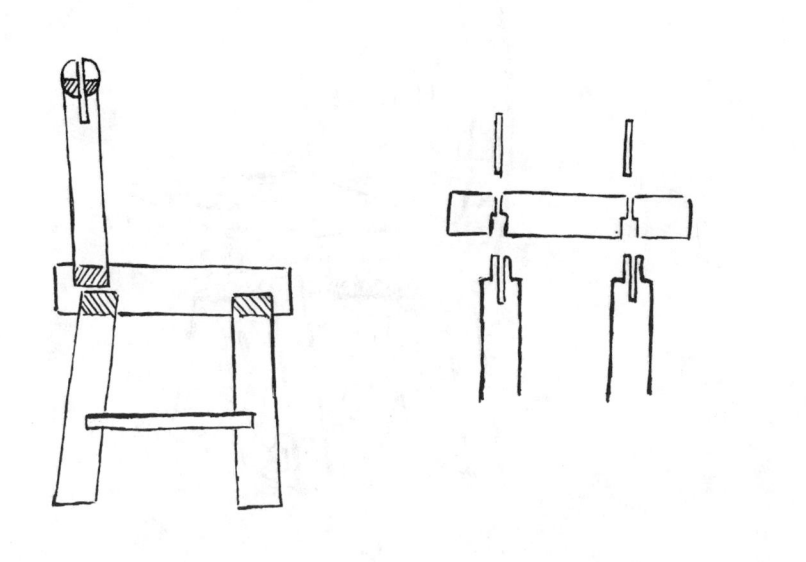

Chair Fifteen

Chair fifteen begins by employing the same two cuts you used to make chair one and several other chairs in this book.

After you have made the first two cuts to achieve the back and seat, take the excess piece you have removed and rip off two slabs about two and one-half inches thick, as shown in the drawing. Now lay the piece to be the back and seat on some supports as shown in the drawing. However, there should be more bracing to keep this piece from rolling.

The two pieces for the legs are not likely to be of the exact same thickness. Instead of using a ruler, trace their width on the bottom of the chair exactly where you want them to be. Now using the method you learned in the section How-to (Slots and Grooves), cut the grooves for the leg installation. Next beat in the legs being sure you have the proper end of the leg in the right slots. Now is the time to carve the protruding parts to fit the chair. The bottom of the legs can now be cut straight to assure an even plane when the chair is set upright for use.

If you are wondering what to do with that last round slab you have left over, you can make the top of an end table or foot stool for the chair.

1.
2.
3.
4.
5.

Chair Sixteen

If you can rip logs and make boards with a relatively large saw and cut curves with a smaller saw, you will have no problem with this chair and hundreds of similar variations.

This chair may be made either thick and heavy or thin and delicate yet still be strong. The back and front piece are fashioned from two slabs of as nearly the same thickness as possible. The seat and leg braces are made of thick dowels or shaved limb wood, all of the same length.

Lining up inserts is explained in the chapter How-to; however I will add a bit for this particular project. Using the end of one of the dowels, trace its circular outline each place you intend to install a dowel on the back piece of the chair. Using the end of your dowel again as a pattern, cut a thin flat sponge into as many circular disks as you have traced circles on the back of the chair. Now paste these sponge disks in the drawn circles on the back of the chair. Next apply ink or paint to these protruding sponges. Be very careful to place the front part of the chair onto the back part of the chair exactly where you want it. In this way, the aligning marker sponges will print correctly on the front piece.

After you have your aligning marks on the front piece, remove the sponges from the back piece. Then drill out all the holes in the marked area. Be sure all the holes are approximately the same depth. They may also be drilled completely through if desired. If there are any signs of marking to be removed before you assemble the chair, now is the time to do it.

To assemble the chair, set the back piece on the floor, glue and install each dowel. Let glue dry. Apply some glue to the protruding dowels. Set the front piece on top of the dowels aligning the holes with the dowels at the same time.

To prevent the chair from twisting while it is drying, nail a temporary brace to the bottom of the legs. A small piece of plywood works fine. If you have no bracing available, stand the chair in a corner in the same position you would be using it—with the back tight against one wall and one side against another. It is possible that no temporary bracing whatsoever will be needed.

A long narrow cushion can be made to cover the seat and the arms as well, with most of the padding being in the seat.

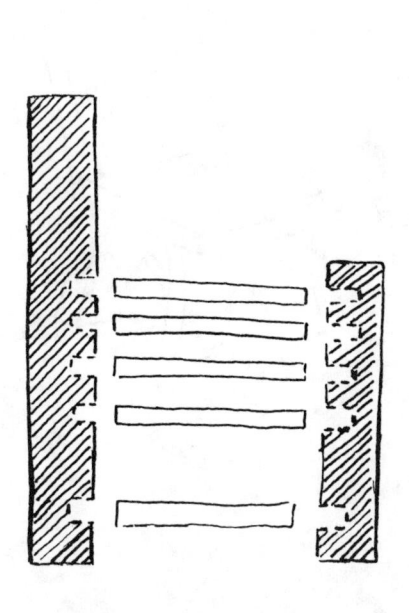

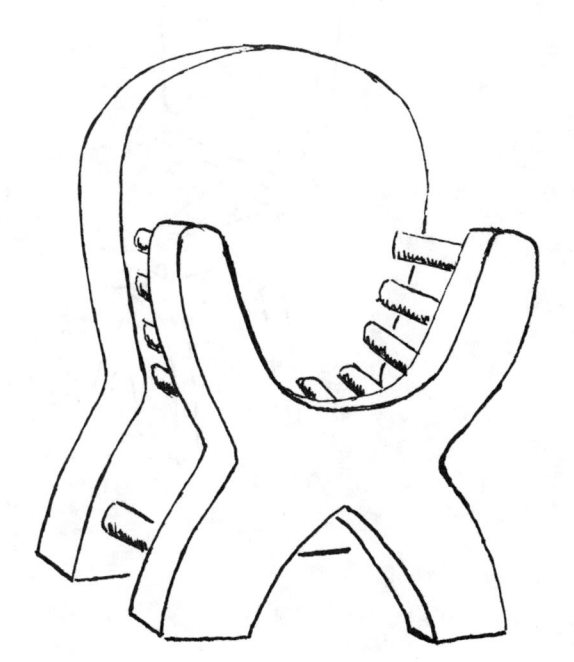

Flat Slab Chairs

These last four chairs have been included to illustrate some of the great variations of style you can achieve with very similar patterns. The top two chairs and one at the bottom right are assembled in exactly the same way. If you are using relatively thin slabs or weak wood, it may be necessary to run a brace from the front legs to the rear legs under the seat. The notch in the back of the chair and the point at which the back of the seat inserts into the back, must meet evenly and squarely. This joint must be glued and doweled from the rear. The front leg will generally stay in well by merely obtaining a firm fit.

The chair at the lower left is of relatively poor design. I have made only one such chair and installed lazy S shaped arms and carved the back slightly. These variations did not seem to improve this design at all. I am including this chair to illustrate that on some of your most creative days you might end up with only some fancy looking firewood, if you don't plan ahead sufficiently.

The only instructions you will need to build these chairs are in the How-to section under Slots and Grooves, Ripping Logs and Making Boards.

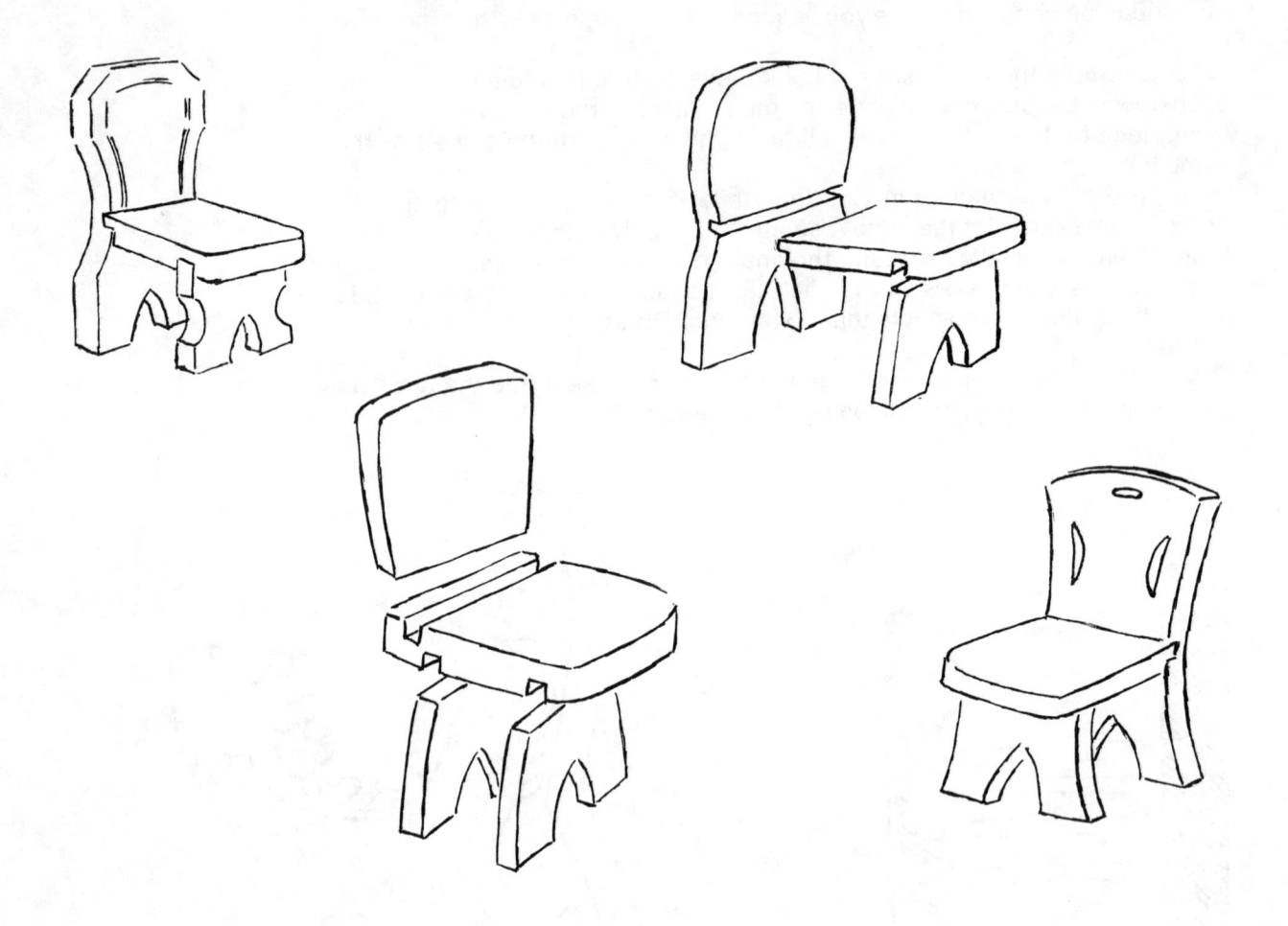

Tables

Table One—Picnic Table

The top of this table is made by ripping a log down the center into two equal parts. The combination table and seat legs are made in almost exactly the same way as chair number one except that the seat is lower to allow for the height of the seat log, and the backs are notched out to fit the table top cross braces.

Before notching the bottom of the table top for the cross braces, lay the two table top pieces flat side down on the ground. Reverse ends of one of these half round logs so as not to have the two pieces come to a V at one end. With the two table top pieces still lying flat side down and the ends flush with one another, take the cross braces and mark their outline on the two half pieces for the top. Notch this outlined area by making numerous cross cuts of desired depth for the cross braces on the table top's underside. After you have notched and fitted the table top for cross braces and legs, notch the underside of the seats to fit the rest of your creation.

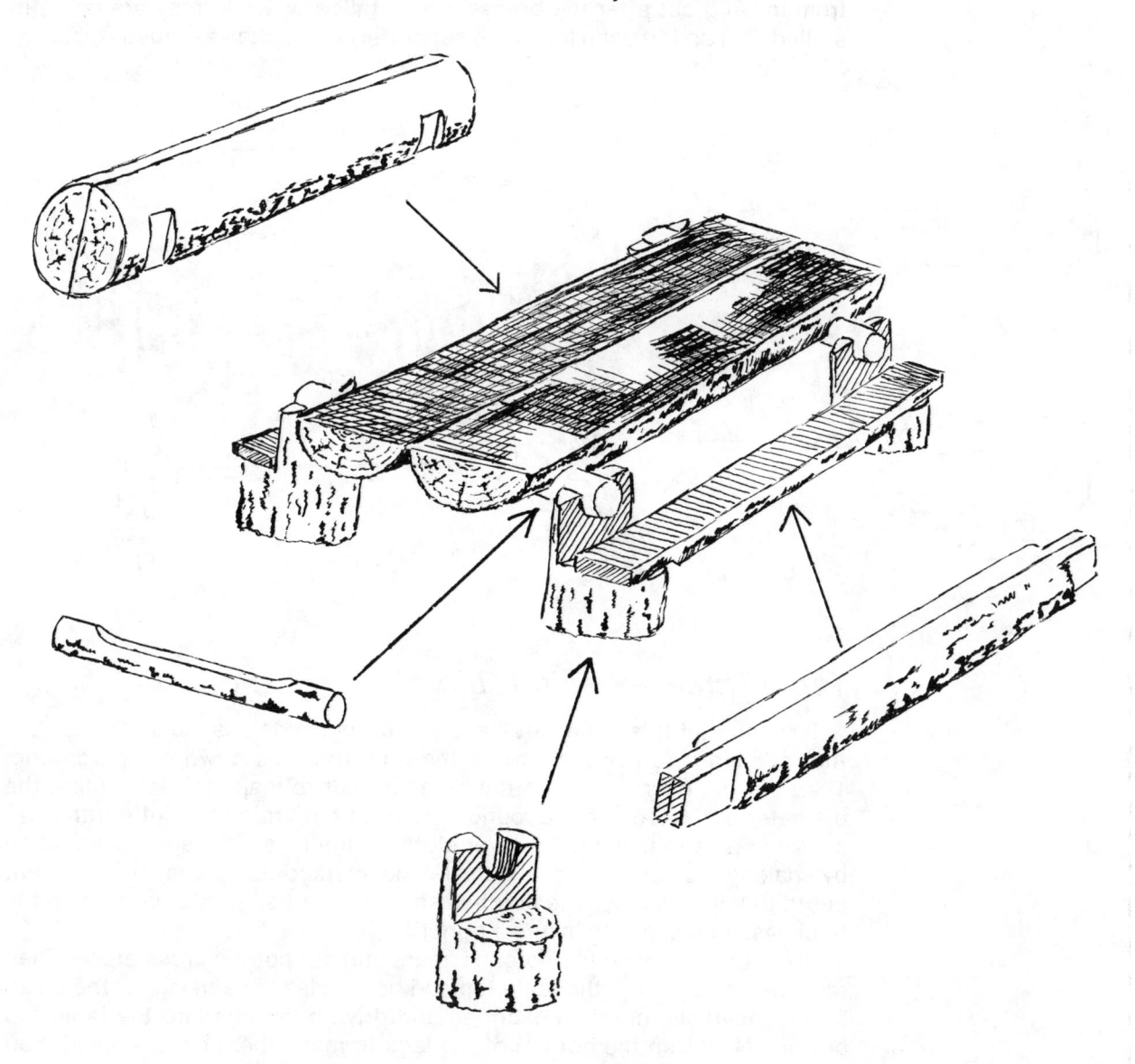

Table Two—Occasional Table

Table two is a very simple table to build if you have a chain saw with a relatively long, straight bar and an evenly sharpened chain to cut the top.

Using a dead, seasoned tree, cut off several six to eight inch thick wafers. Pick the best one for your table top. Lay the top face down on some logs to protect your bar and chain while you make three or four plunge cuts for the leg hole.

Make plunge cuts and install the legs as you did on chair number three, except that the holes need to be bored completely through the table top. After the legs are installed and the table set right side up, you can drive wedges into the slots just as you would to secure an axe head to an axe handle. If the table does not sit flat on the ground, tip it upside down again and make the necessary adjustments by trimming each leg. The braces are optional. If your table legs fit the top tightly and if the legs slant properly, the table will not need leg braces. If you do wish to install braces, it is most easily done when the table is sitting right side up. Knock each leg as far as it will go toward the outer edge of the table top. This is to prevent the legs from moving out after the braces are installed or while they are being installed. Cut and fit each leg brace separately and install as illustrated.

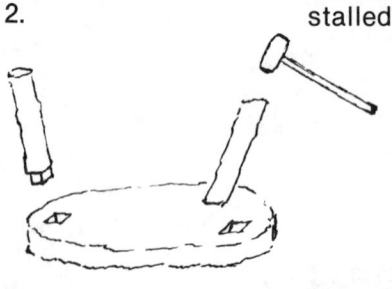

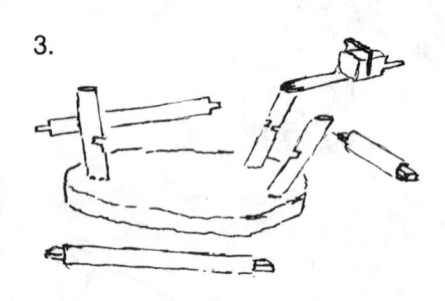

Table Three—Picnic Table

To construct this table, cut two slabs off one side of a log as shown. Lay the rounded side (which is to be the top), flat side down on the ground. Then cut the piece with two flat sides in half to make the legs. Mark the diameter of the legs on the round bottom of the table top. Cut out the two marked areas to make notches or slots for the legs. These slots are made by making numerous cross cuts in the marked-out areas, of sufficient depth to hold the legs. The notches should be cut slightly smaller than the thickness of the legs to insure a tight fit.

Now set the legs in the notches, mark and cut out the cross brace. Then remove the legs from the table top and bore holes in each leg for the cross brace. Insert the brace in each leg and drive both legs into the table top bottom. Now trim the bottom of the legs to make them flat and even. You may now carve the legs to suit your taste.

Table Three—Method

Table Four—Coffee Table

This table is made from three separate logs. Begin the top of the table by making two oblique cuts in the log about four or five inches apart. A good idea is to cut five or six wafers, as illustrated, off the same log. Choose the one with the best grain pattern and craftsmanship in cutting.

The two legs are made by making three rip cuts in another log, as illustrated. Square off the two leg blocks, then cut and carve to suit your taste. Cut notches for the cross braces. The cross brace is made by removing three sides of a small log, then notching it out to fit the notches in the top of the table legs at the best length for stability and aesthetics. The legs and cross braces may be fastened together either by the use of pegs or glue. The table top may be fastened onto the legs in the same manner.

Table Four—Method

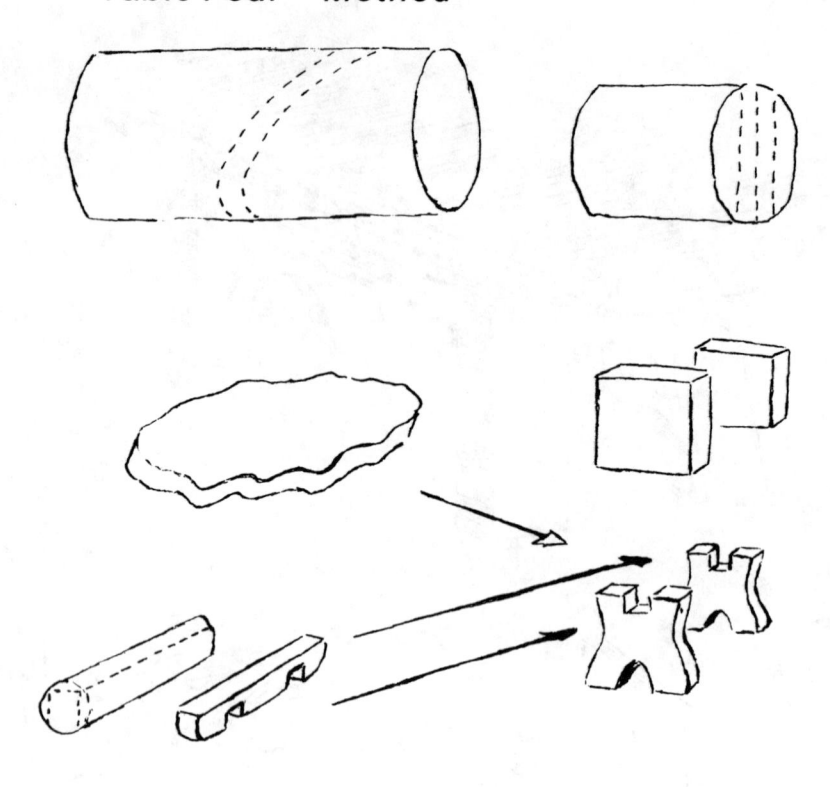

Tables Five, Six and Seven

These tables are basically the same. They all may be built of small logs. They can all be achieved with the smallest chain saws on the market, providing the chain is properly sharpened, the bar is straight, the spark plug and air filter are clean, and the saw is otherwise mechanically sound and functioning as it was meant to.

Gather two or more straight logs six to eight feet long and ten to twelve inches in diameter. Rip these logs lengthwise, the flat sides will be the top of the table. Trim and straighten the outer edges of the half round pieces with your saw to assure a snug fit when the table is assembled. It may be beneficial to mention at this time that it would be best to rip more than two or three logs for the table top, because if you rip six or eight, you will have a better choice. You can always use the extra pieces for other projects, parts of this project, or firewood. Keep in mind you will probably want to make matching benches.

Now that you have the table top cut, place the pieces on a flat surface, flat side down and laying side by side in the tightest, squarest fashion possible. It might be best to temporarily nail the top down with a few old boards or slabs to keep all parts aligned.

Cut one log the same length as the width of the table top. Rip this log lengthwise to make cross braces. Lay the cross braces on the bottom of the table top where you want them. Trace the outline of each brace on the bottom of the table top. Remove the cross braces. Cut out slots for the cross braces, referring to the section Slots and Grooves in the chapter How-to. Build the rest of the table using these illustrated designs or others you may design yourself. There are also other designs in this book which you could use.

Table Five—Method

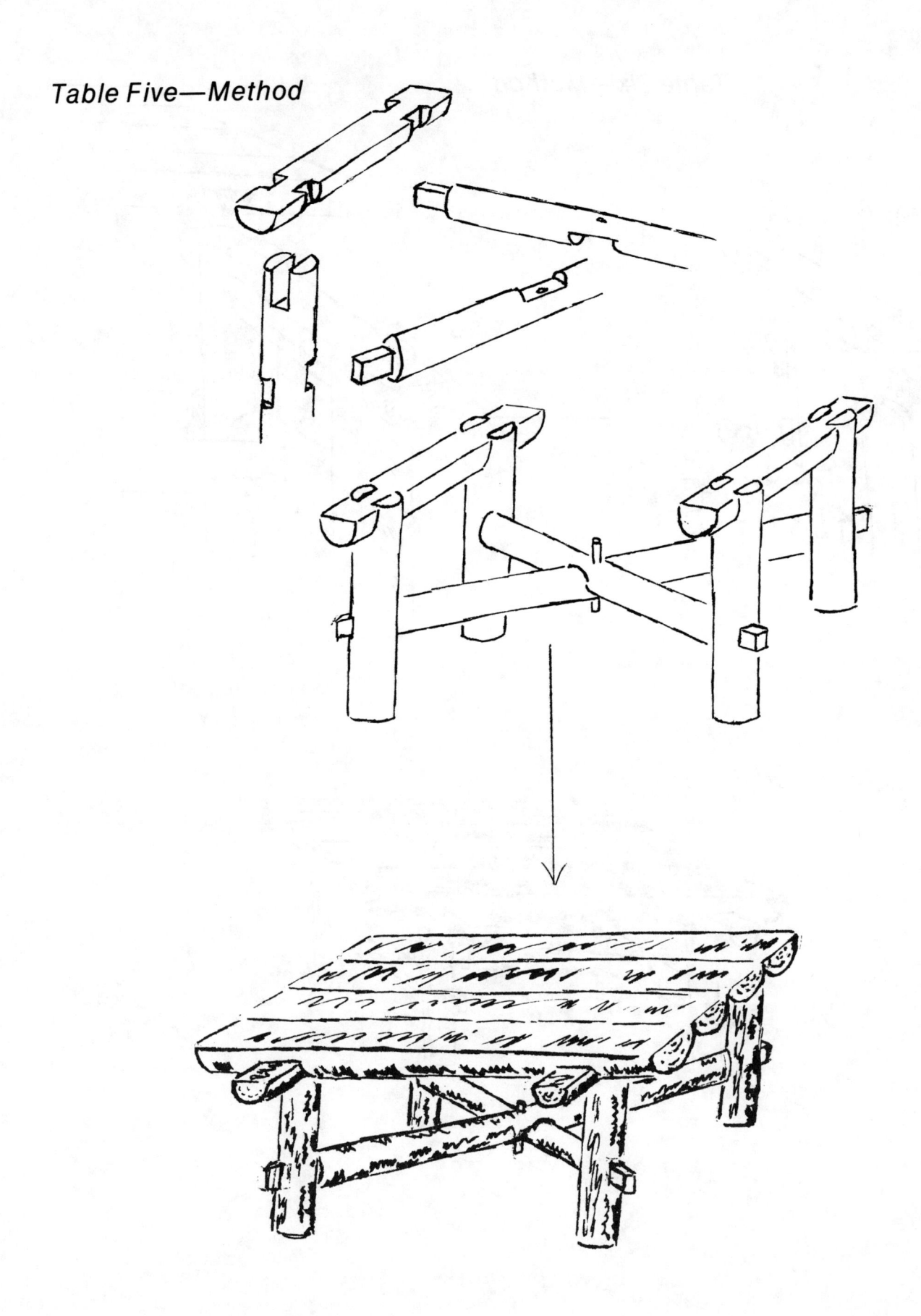

Table Six—Method

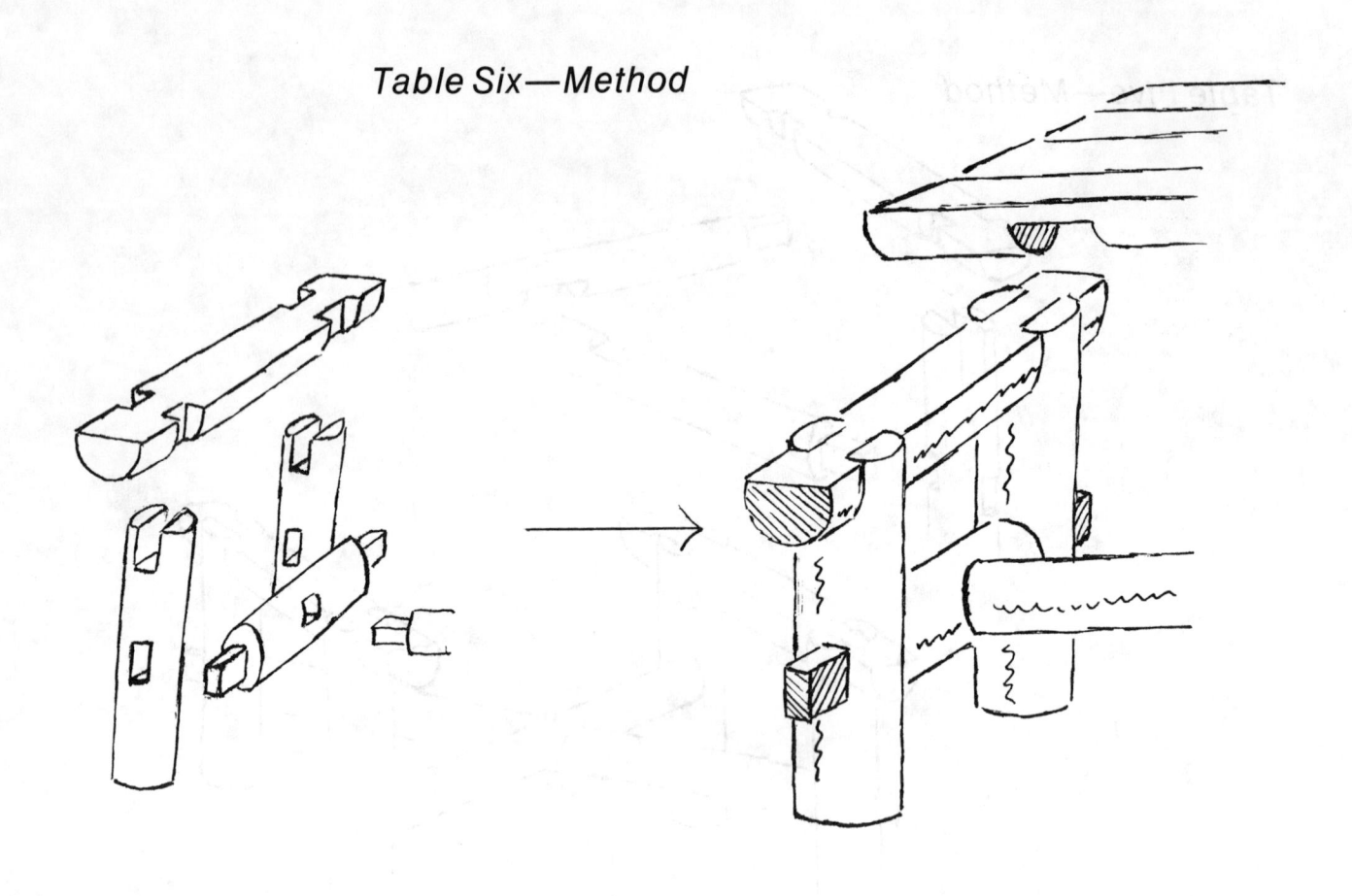

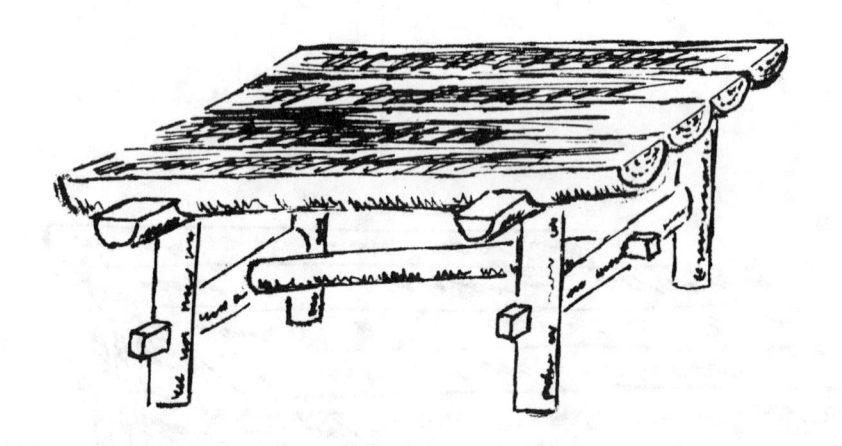

Table Seven—Method

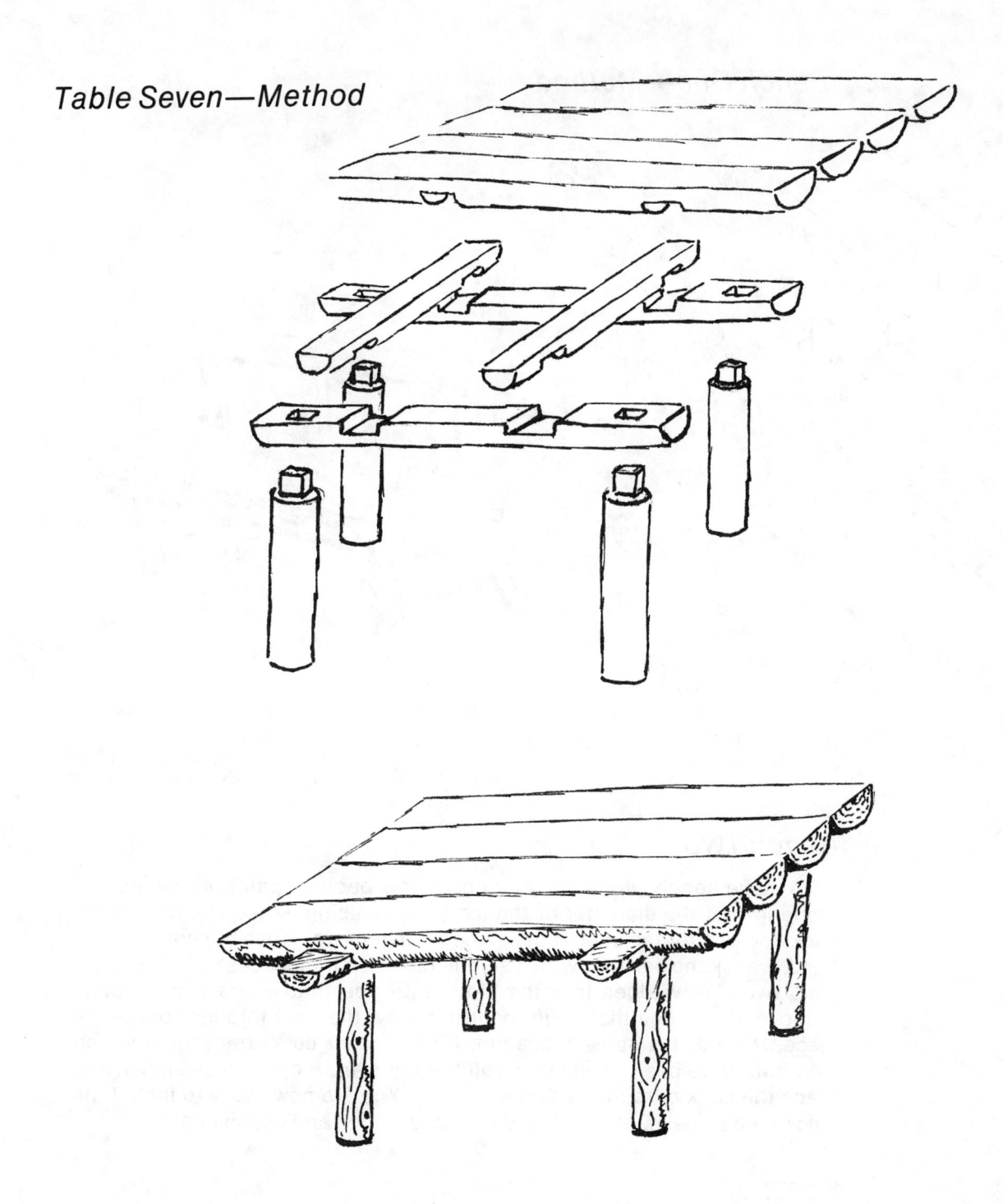

Benches

Bench One

Bench one will offer little difficulty if you have made chair three, since both utilize the same basic construction. The seat of the bench is made by merely ripping a log of desired width and length down the middle.

The leg holes are made the same way as explained in the text for chair three. There are numerous ways to make back braces, as shown in the accompanying illustration.

Bench One—Method

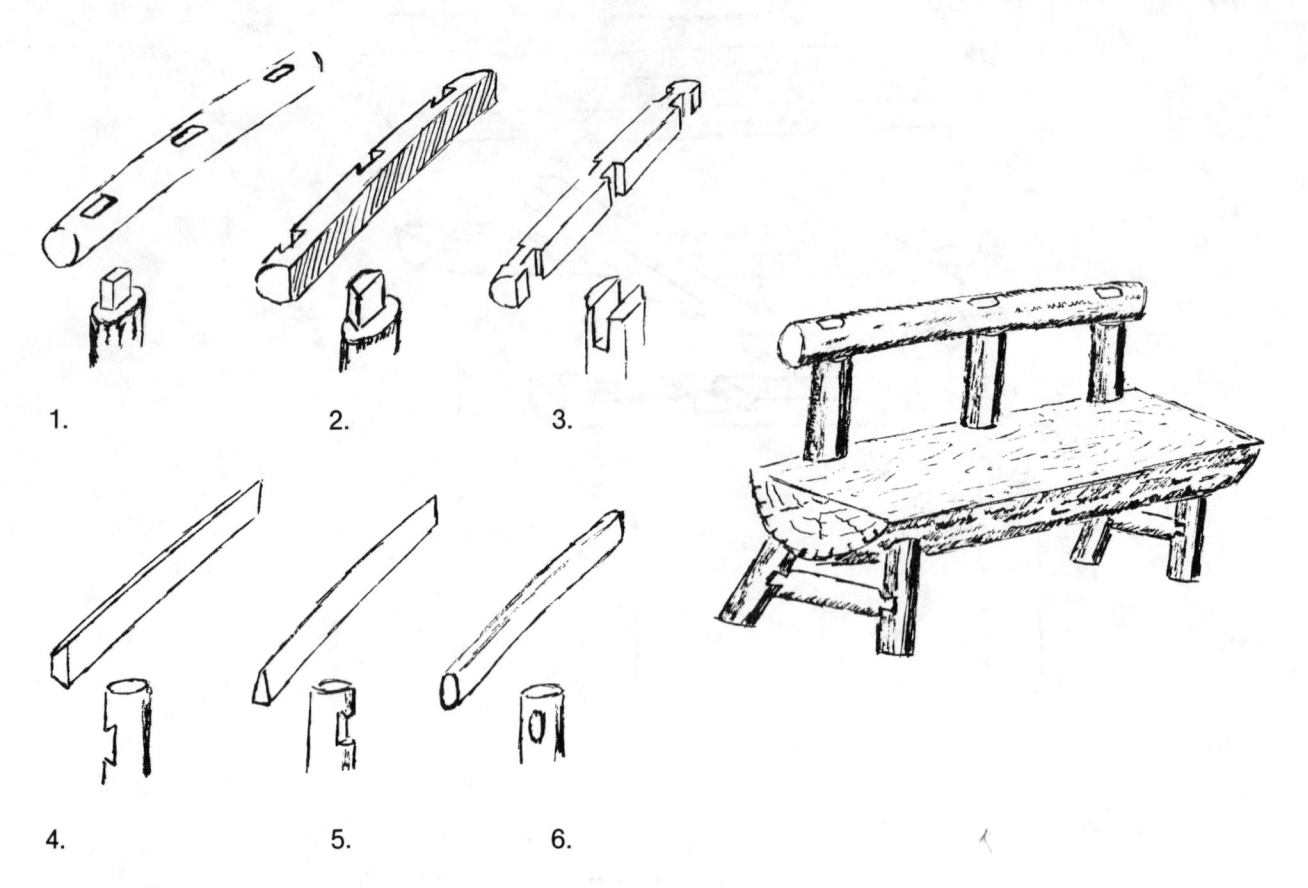

1.
2.
3.
4.
5.
6.

Bench Two

To make bench two, mark your chain saw bar with paint or crayon, half the length of the diameter of the log you are using. Make one cut for the back and one for the seat. If the piece to be removed does not come out by hand, whack the end of it with a sledge hammer. If this does not work, drive small wooden wedges into the slots until you find where it is holding. Remove any wedge that might be in the way, then cut through to free the piece. Repeat this same procedure for the other cut. After the back and seat cuts have been completed, roll the log over. Prop it up as shown and brace the back or rounded side of the log. You are now ready to install the legs in the same manner as you did on chair three and bench one.

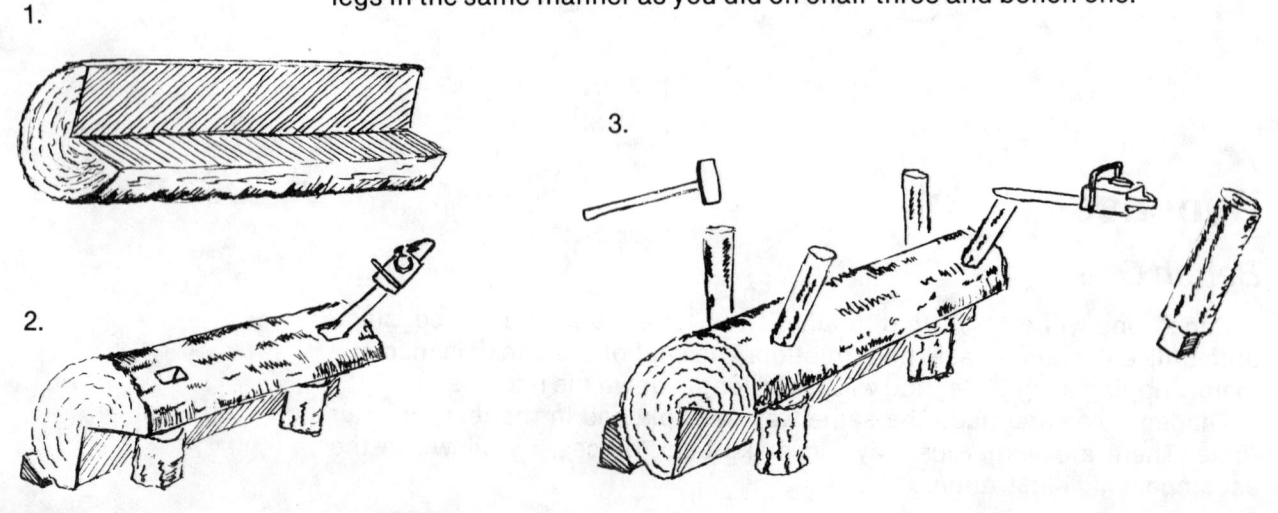

1.
2.
3.

Completed view of Bench Two

Armed Bench

To make the armed bench, choose a log of sufficient length and diameter. Cut off two sides of the log equally, then roll the log with one of the flat sides down. Mark the ends at the desired height of the arm from the ground and the desired length of the arms from the front of the bench to the front of the seat. Remove this block and complete the arms, back and seat, as shown. If you should run into trouble removing this last block, refer to instructions for bench two.

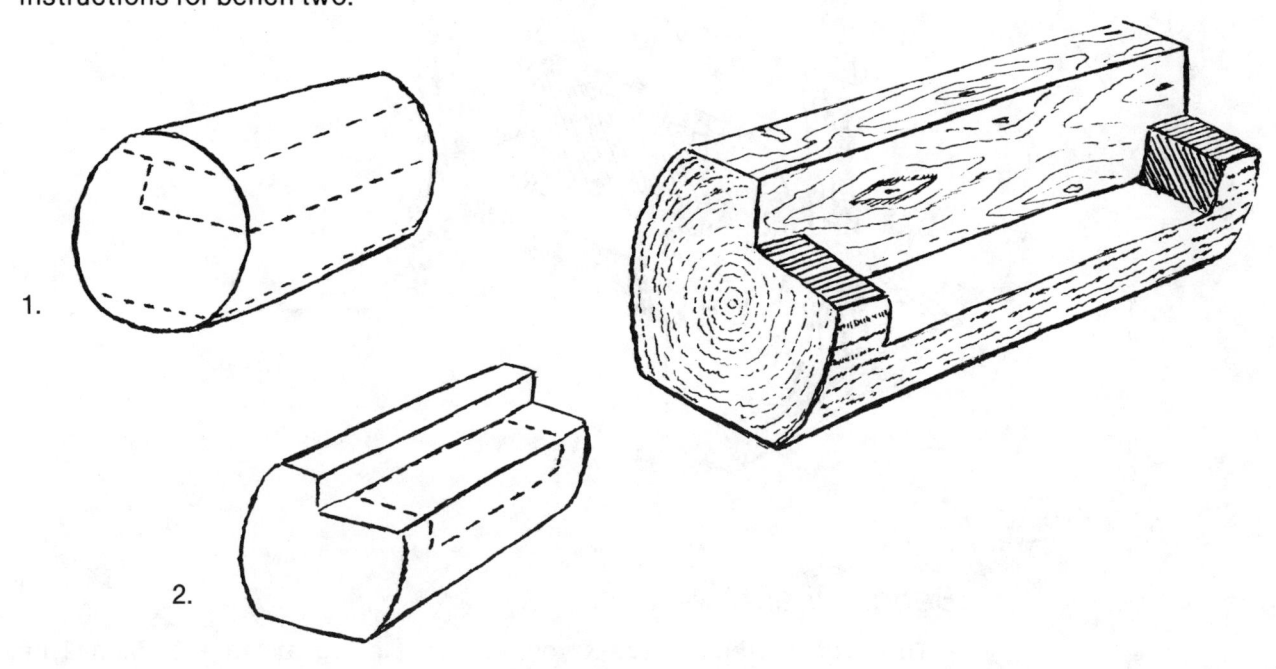

1.

2.

Swing Bench

The swing bench is made in almost the same way as the armed bench, except that the bottom need not be flat. The illustration of the braced frame is self-explanatory.

If the frame is made of some strong wood, such as red oak, it will easily hold a light conifer seat. If the entire structure is made solely of conifer, the bottom brace must be tied to the upper brace to assure enough strength in the frame to support the weight of the seat and its users.

Swing Bench—Method

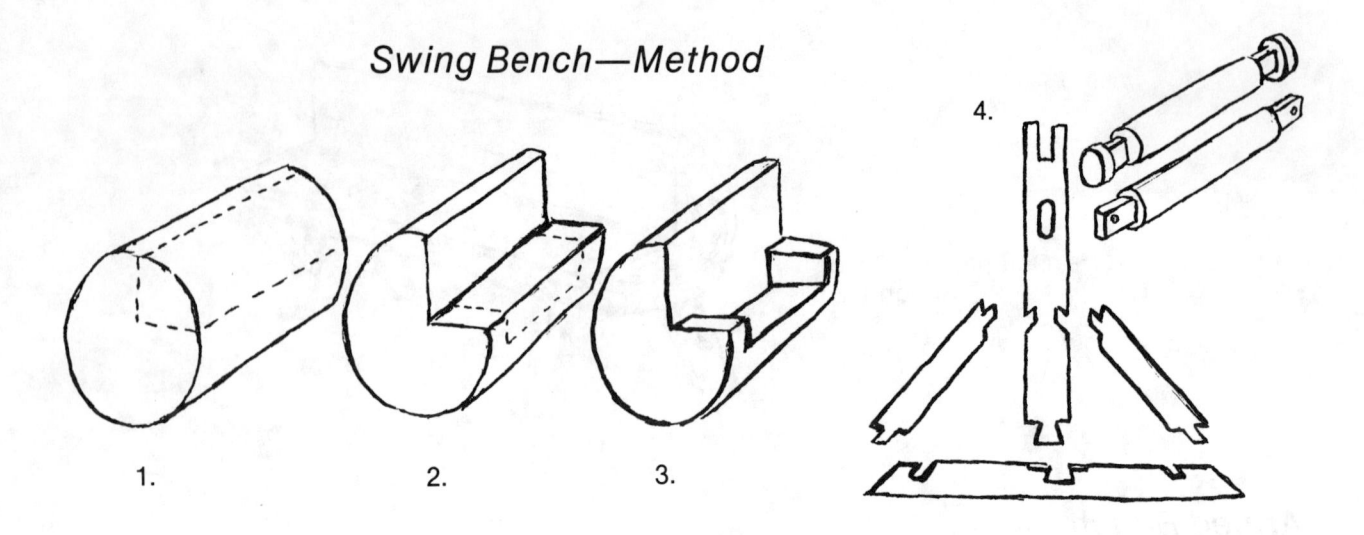

1.
2.
3.
4.

Bench Chest

To make this bench chest you will want a log at least 20 inches in diameter and long enough to suit the place you are going to put it.

Study the illustration carefully. The log will have to be ripped in three places. The first cut is made where the top of the seat lid will be. The second cut will remove the seat from the main chest. The third cut will remove the floor or bottom of the chest.

The hollowed portion is cut from the main body of the chest by outlining the rectangle to be removed. Plunge cut along these lines. For a neat job, cut the corners last. Use at least four bracing logs when making these plunge cuts.

To reassemble the chest, glue or peg the floor of the chest to the main body or hollowed out portion. Then install the desired type of legs. Turn the bench right side up and fasten on the lid/seat with metal or leather hinges.

To install a backrest, make two dovetailed slots in the main body of the chest. Rip a small log down the center to use as uprights. Dovetail one end of the piece to fit the dovetailed slots. For the backrest itself, you can rip the side off a small log. Cut dovetail slots in the uprights and install the backrest from one end, or you can use one of the methods shown for bench one.

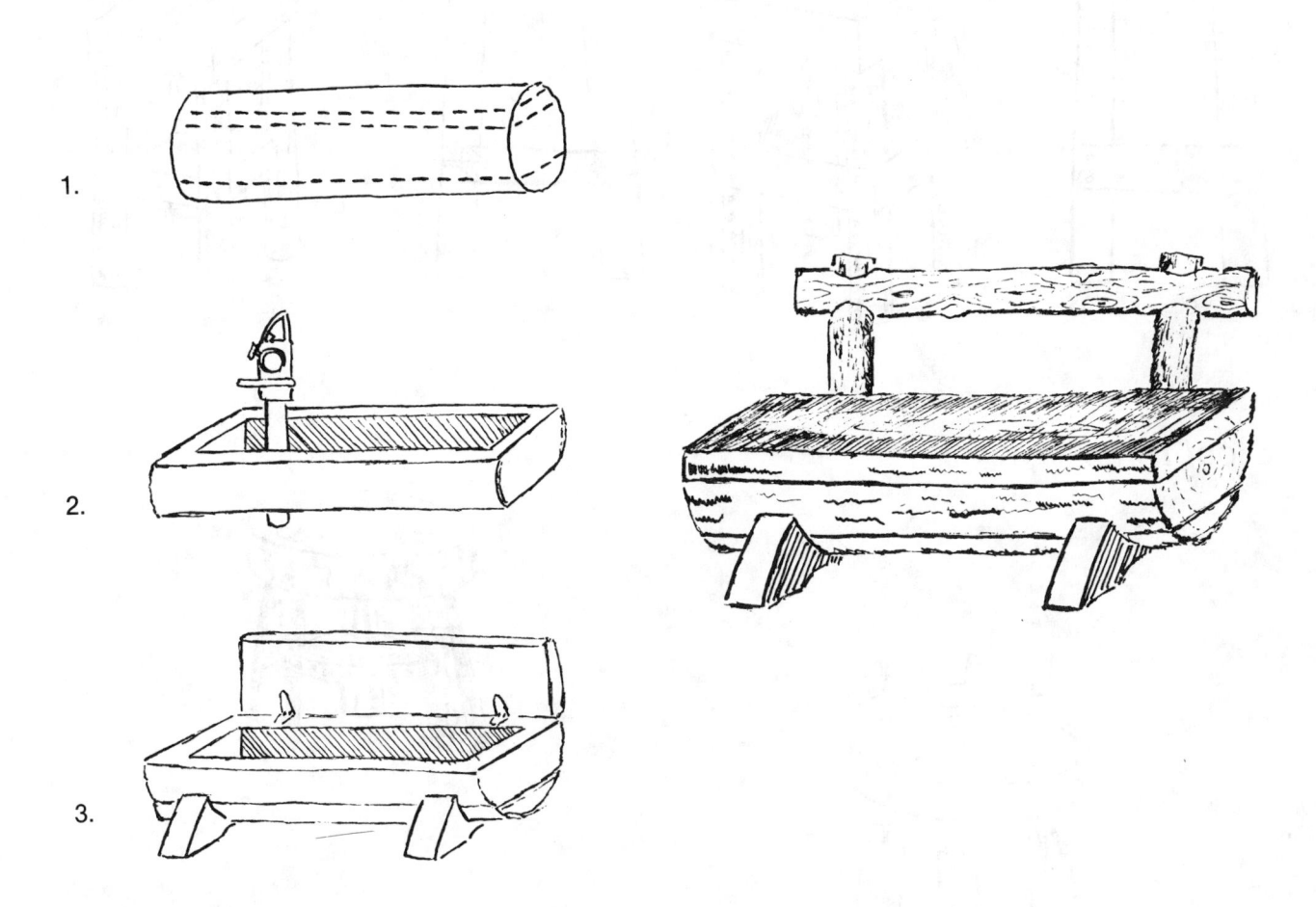

1.

2.

3.

Stools

There are many stools illustrated in this section, some with seats cut across the grain in wafer fashion. If you plan on using this design, you will have to find a well-seasoned, crackless log of tight, hard fiber. The seats made of slabs cut with the grain can be made of almost any variety of wood in good, sound condition with slabs sufficiently thick.

The bark can be peeled off the legs before you trace the outline of the legs on the bottom of the seat. After the legs are traced on the bottom of the seat, drill a series of holes just inside the perimeter of the traced area. Remove the wood inside this area with a gouge and mallet. Install the legs before bracing them. If you should have any difficulty constructing these stools, read the How-to section (Round holes and Slots) for more detailed information.

Seat cushions can be made of foam rubber or with various types of stuffing inserted in appropriate sized cushion covers. Consult the section on Couches for more information on how to construct cushions. There is also some helpful information in the Beds section under mattresses.

Stool One

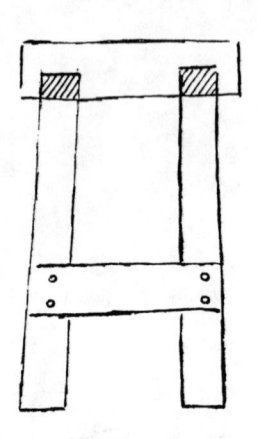

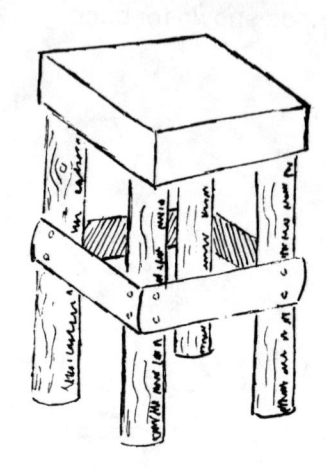

Stool Two

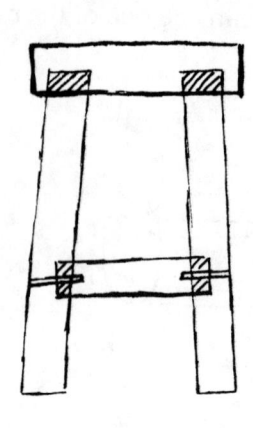

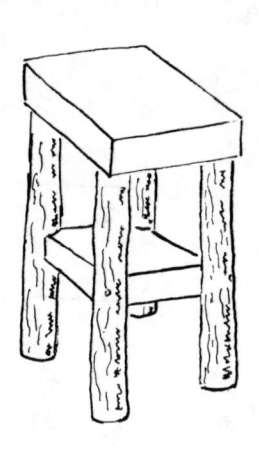

Stool Three

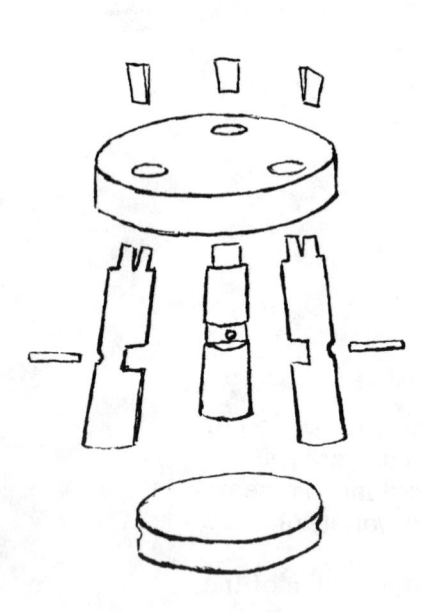

or

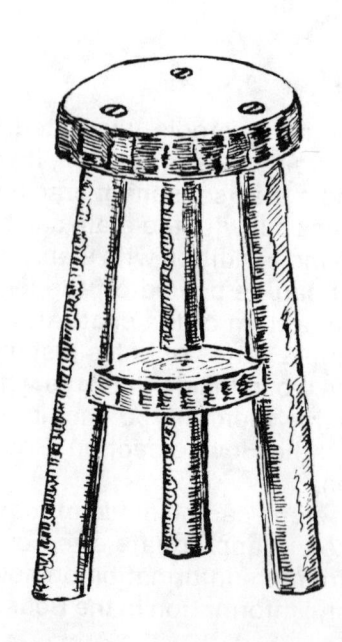

Stool Four

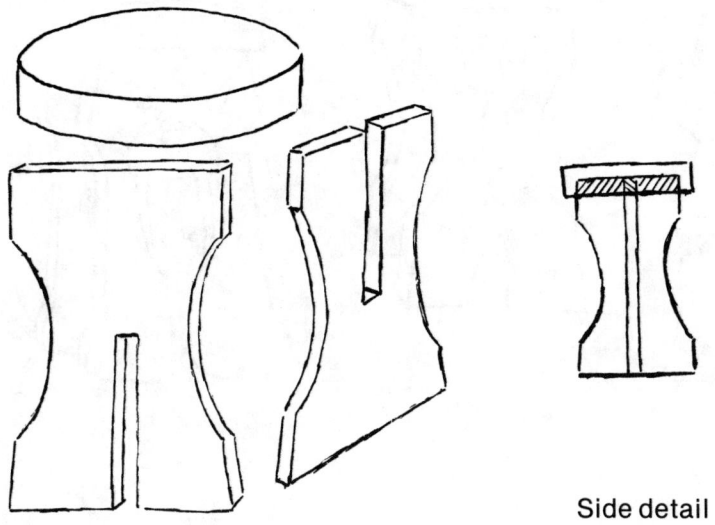

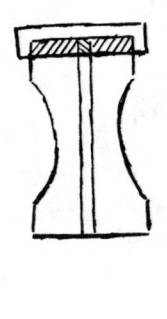

Side detail

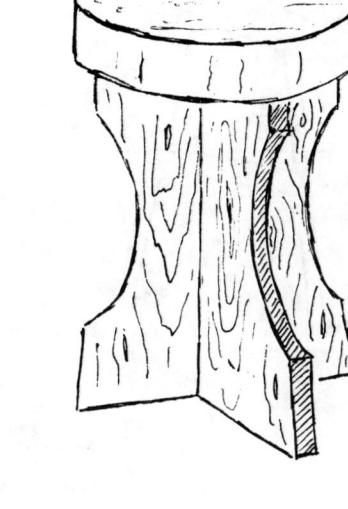

Stool Five

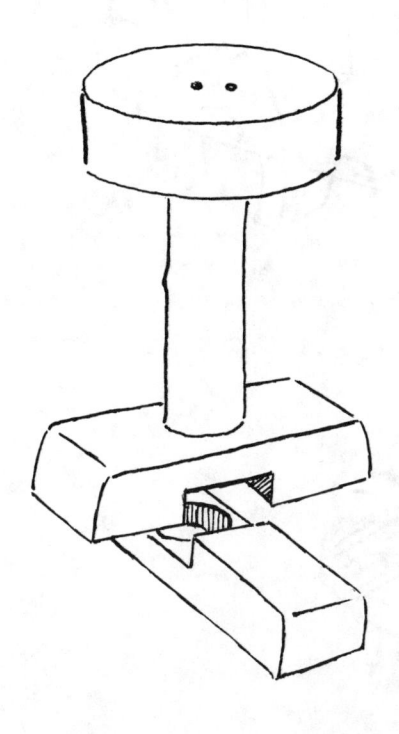

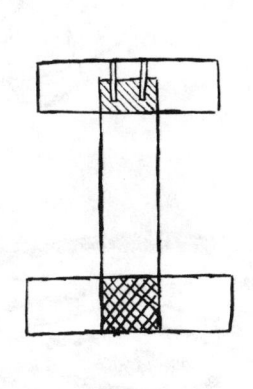

Side detail

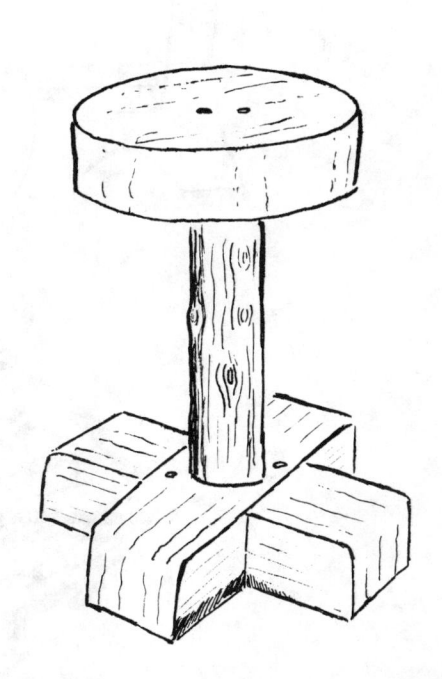

69

Additional Stools

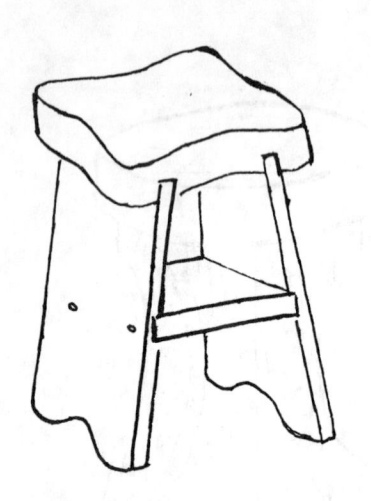

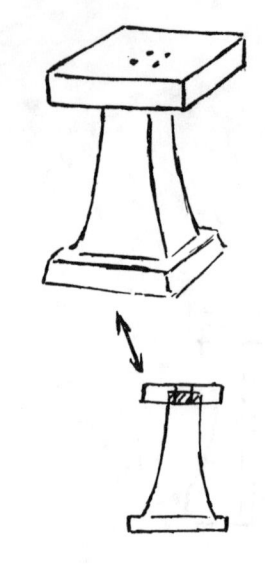

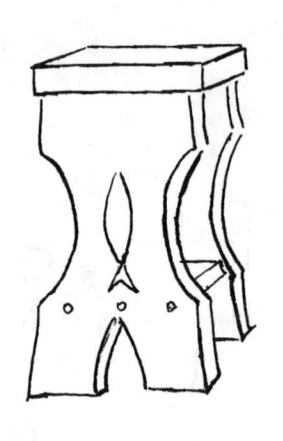

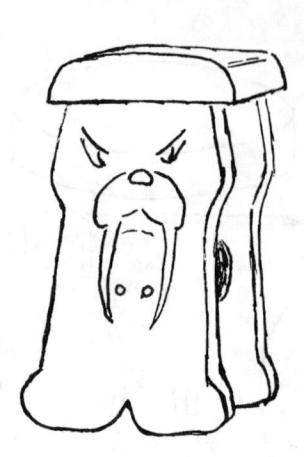

Couches

The three basic designs of chain saw built couches are relatively simple to build, if you have studied the How-to section and have built a few of the chairs in this book. The basic techniques reuired here have been covered in earlier projects, so it should not be difficult to build these couches.

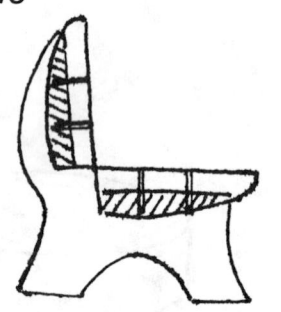

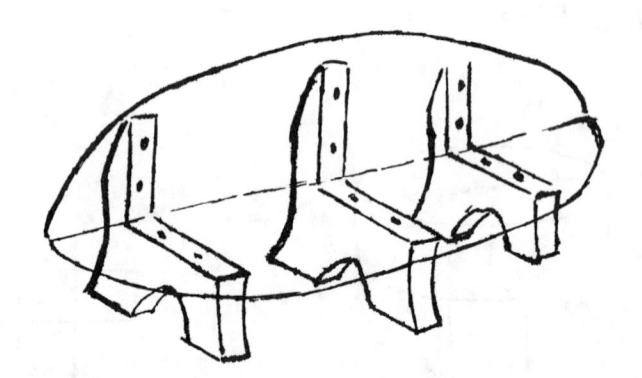

Couch One

Couch Two

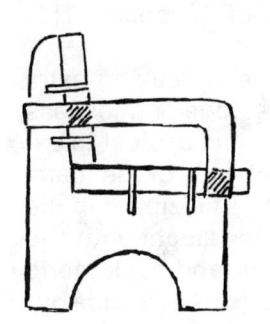

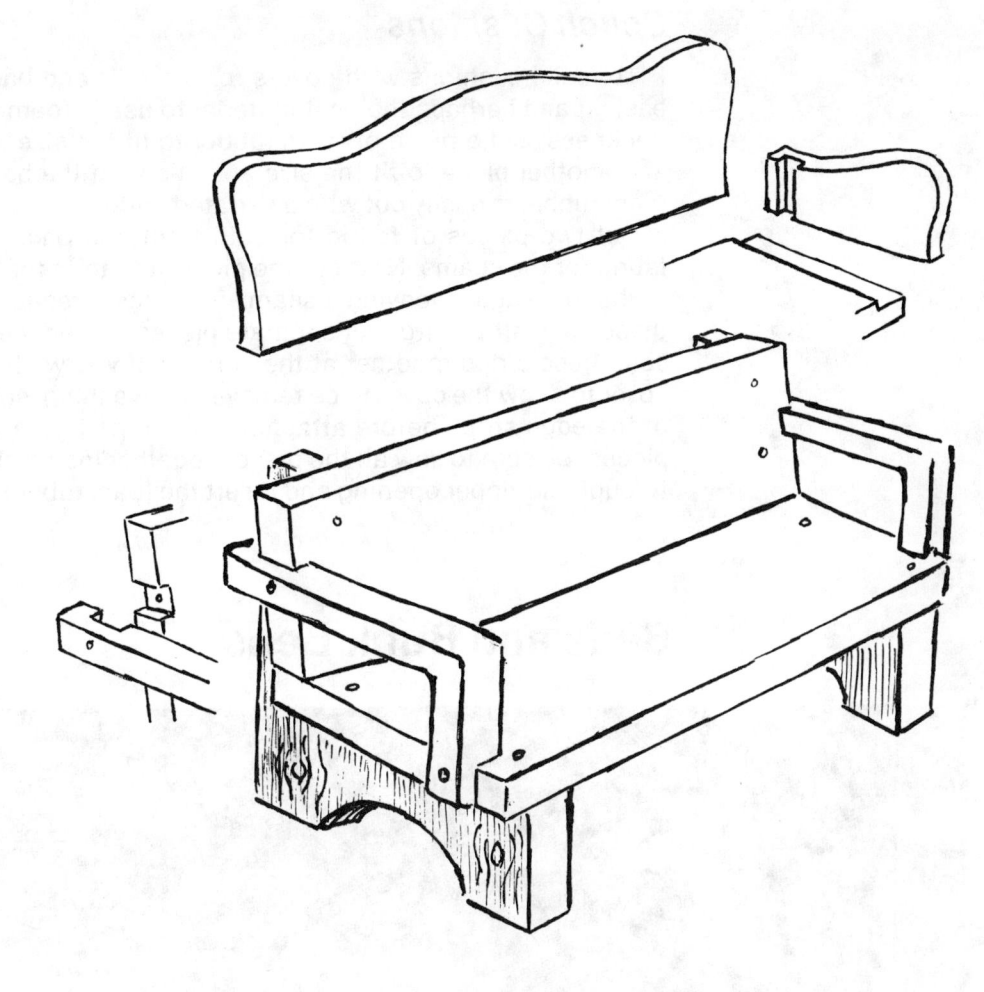

Couch Three

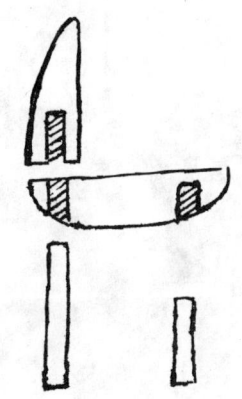

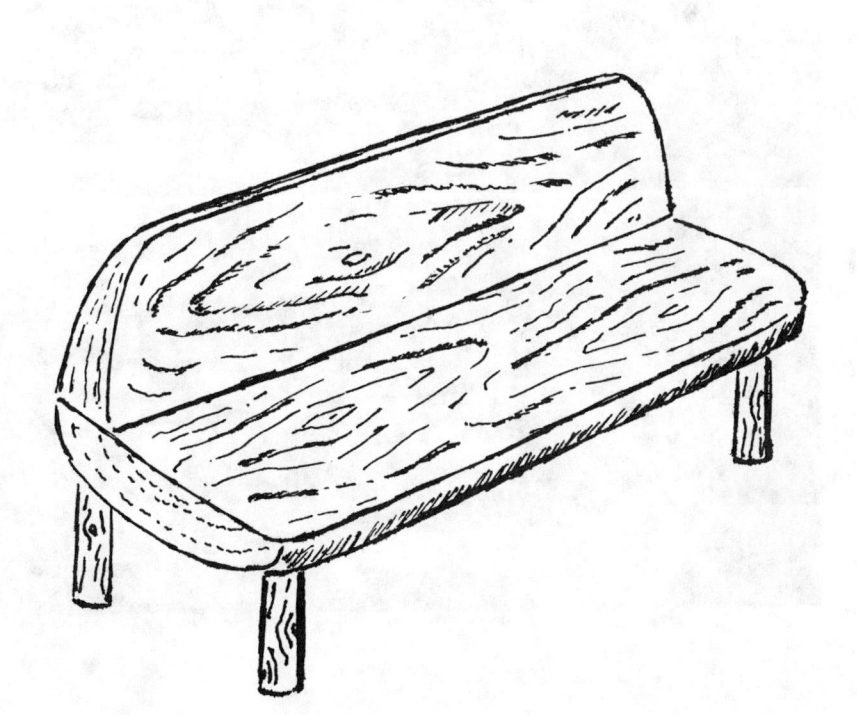

71

Couch Cushions

To make cushions with covers for the seat and back of your couch, the easiest and perhaps the best material to use is foam rubber of any desired thickness. Cut a piece of foam rubber to fit the size and shape of the seat and another piece to fit the size and shape of the back of the couch. This foam rubber is easily cut with a serrated knife.

Cut two pieces of fabric for both front and back pieces, leaving extra fabric for the seams. Now cut the pieces of fabric for the edge or thickness of the foam again, leaving a seam allowance. Frequently it is easiest to cut these edge strips into four separate pieces—one for each side of the foam. Join these strips together at the corners. If you wish to put a zipper in the cover to allow the cover to be removed for washing, sew the zipper onto one of the edge strips before attaching the strips to the front and back fabric pieces. Be sure to sew all the pieces together inside out. Turn right side out through the zipper opening and insert the foam rubber.

Beds and Bunk Beds

The illustration on beds and bunk beds is mostly self-explanatory. The skills needed to achieve these projects are explained in the How-to section. As with the couches, you should experience no difficulty with these projects.

If you are going to use conventional box springs and mattresses, you will have to plan for a specific size mattress and spring. However, if you are going to use rope, cross woven back and forth to take the place of the box springs, you can make the bed plans according to your size. This is great for people over six feet tall who are generally hanging over the end of the bed.

Another substitute for box springs may be fashioned from woven scrub willow or other flexible tree boughs to make a matt. Thin cottonwood and elm boards can also be woven into matts. A well stretched elk or moose hide laced to the outer perimeter of the bed is also quite suitable. A stout canvas tarp with enough grommets works well. Plywood can also be used over cross members.

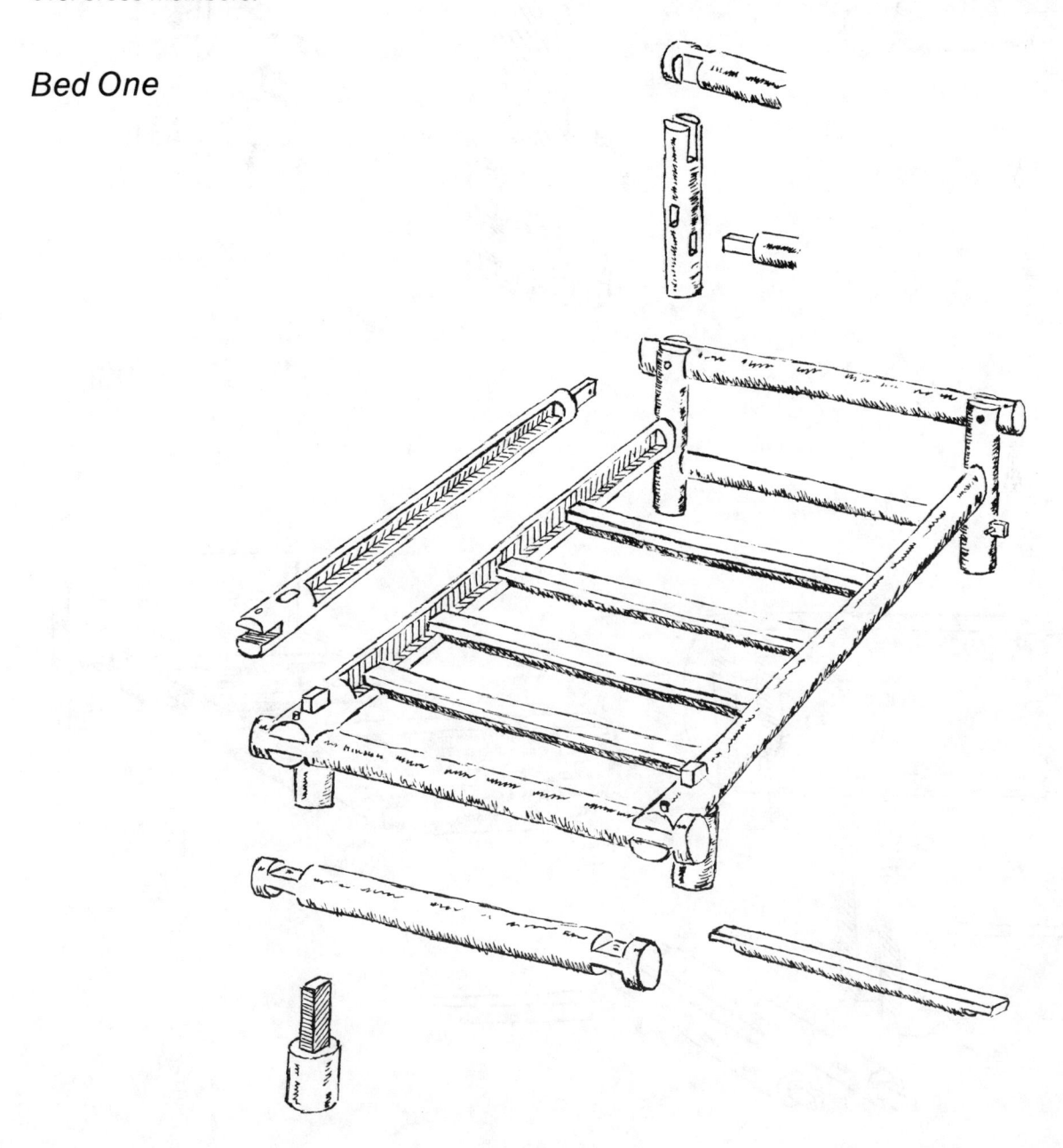

Bed One

Bed Two

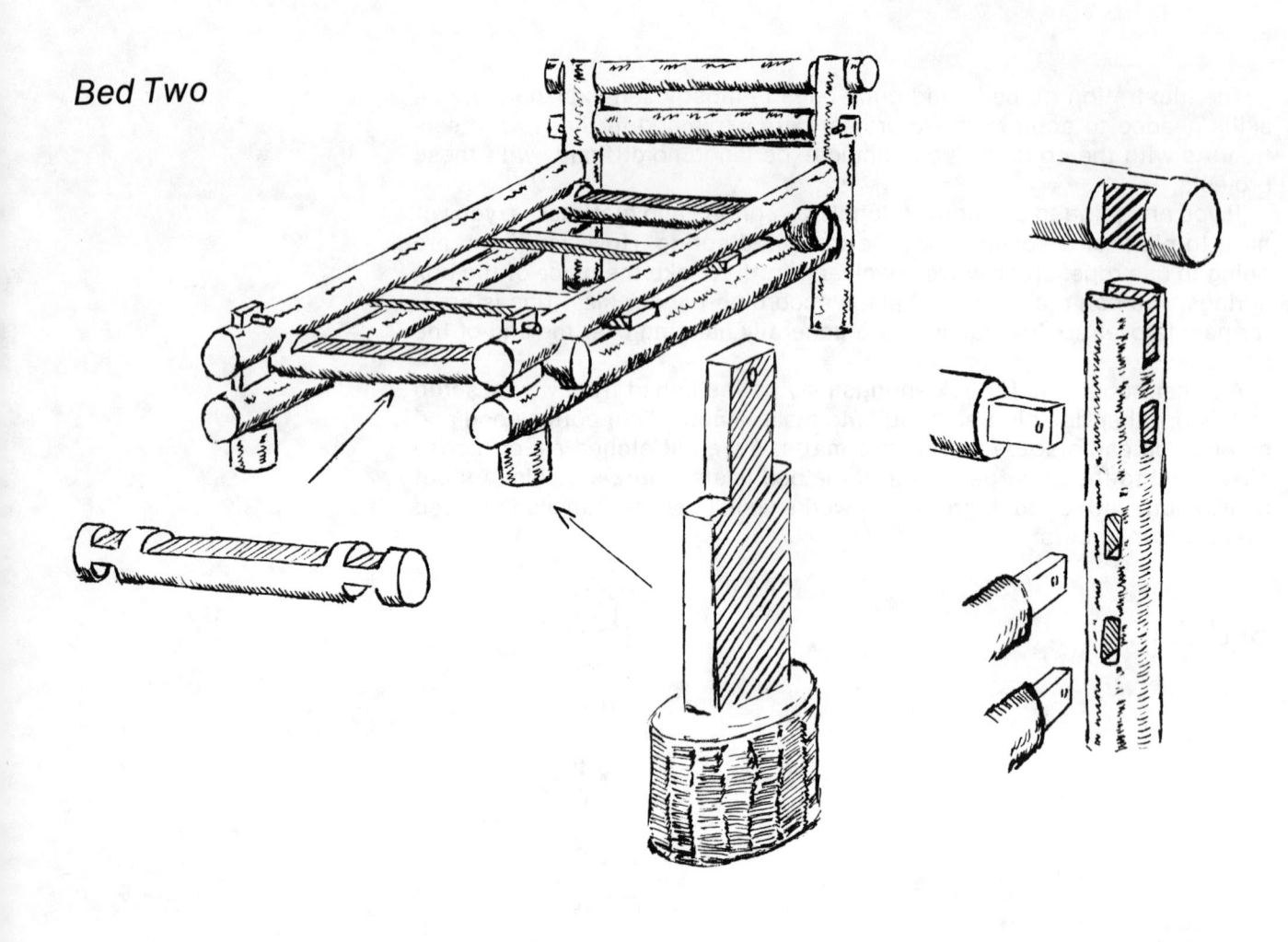

Bed Three

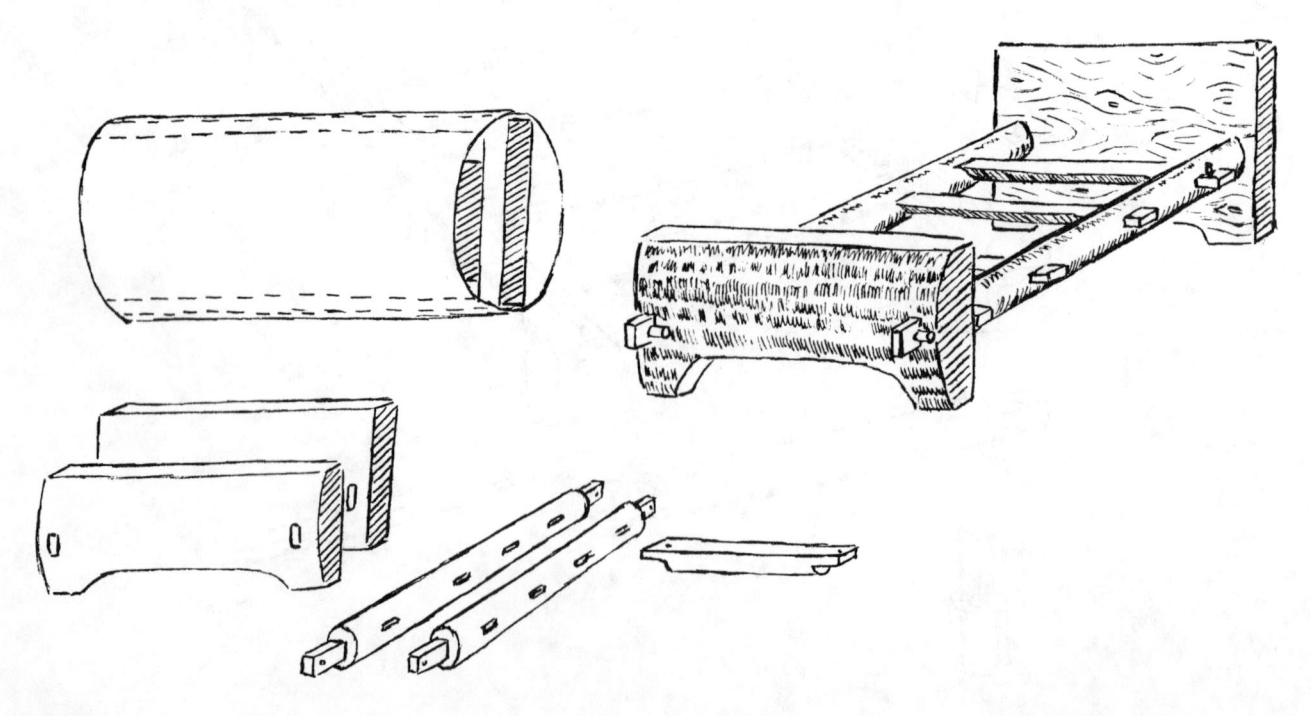

Bed Four

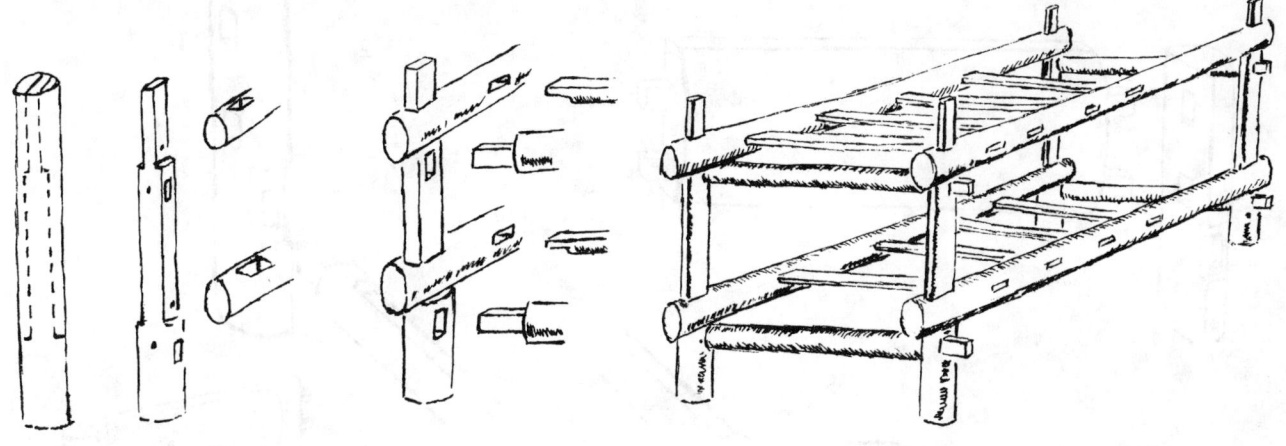

Bed Five

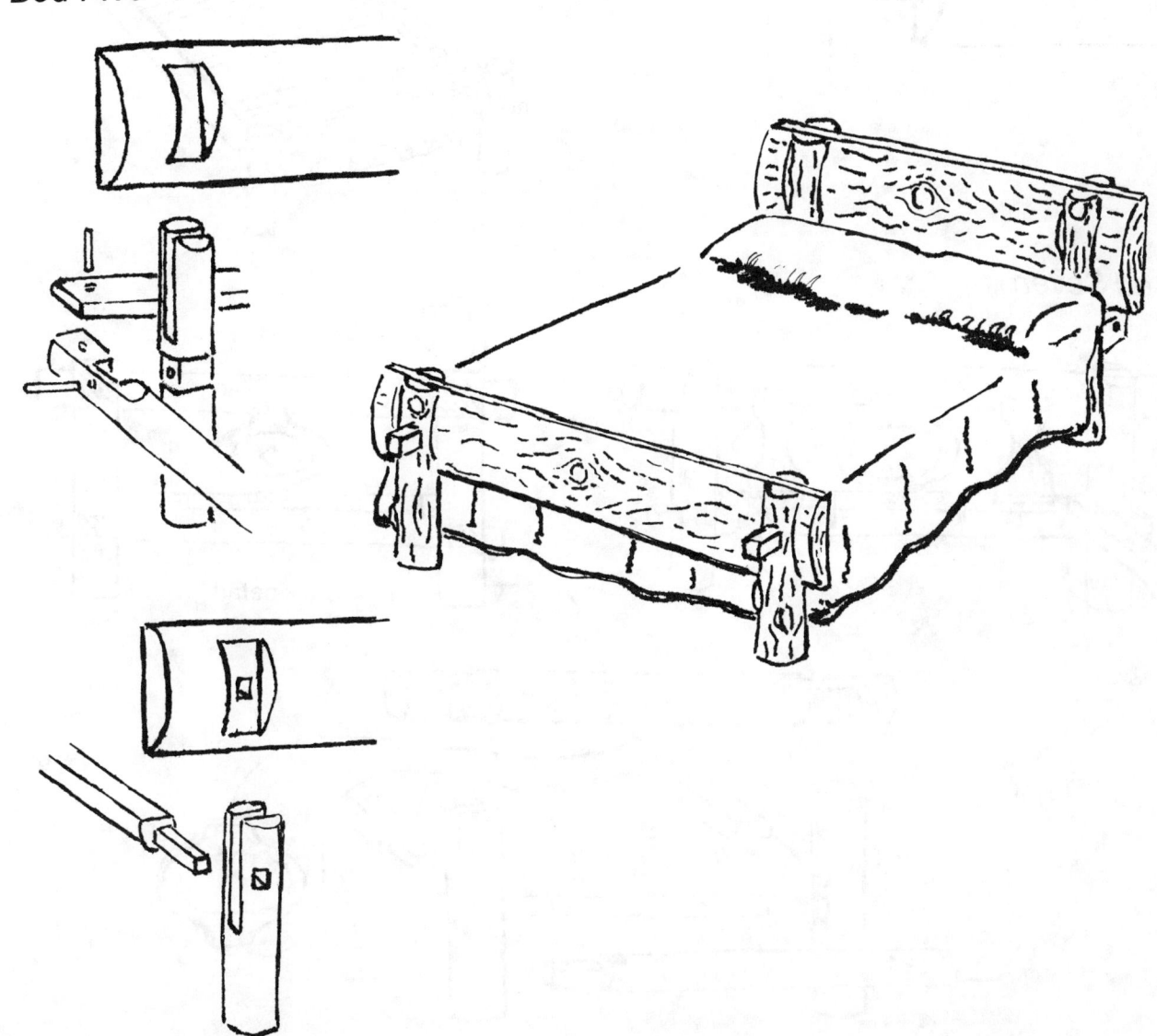

Bed Six

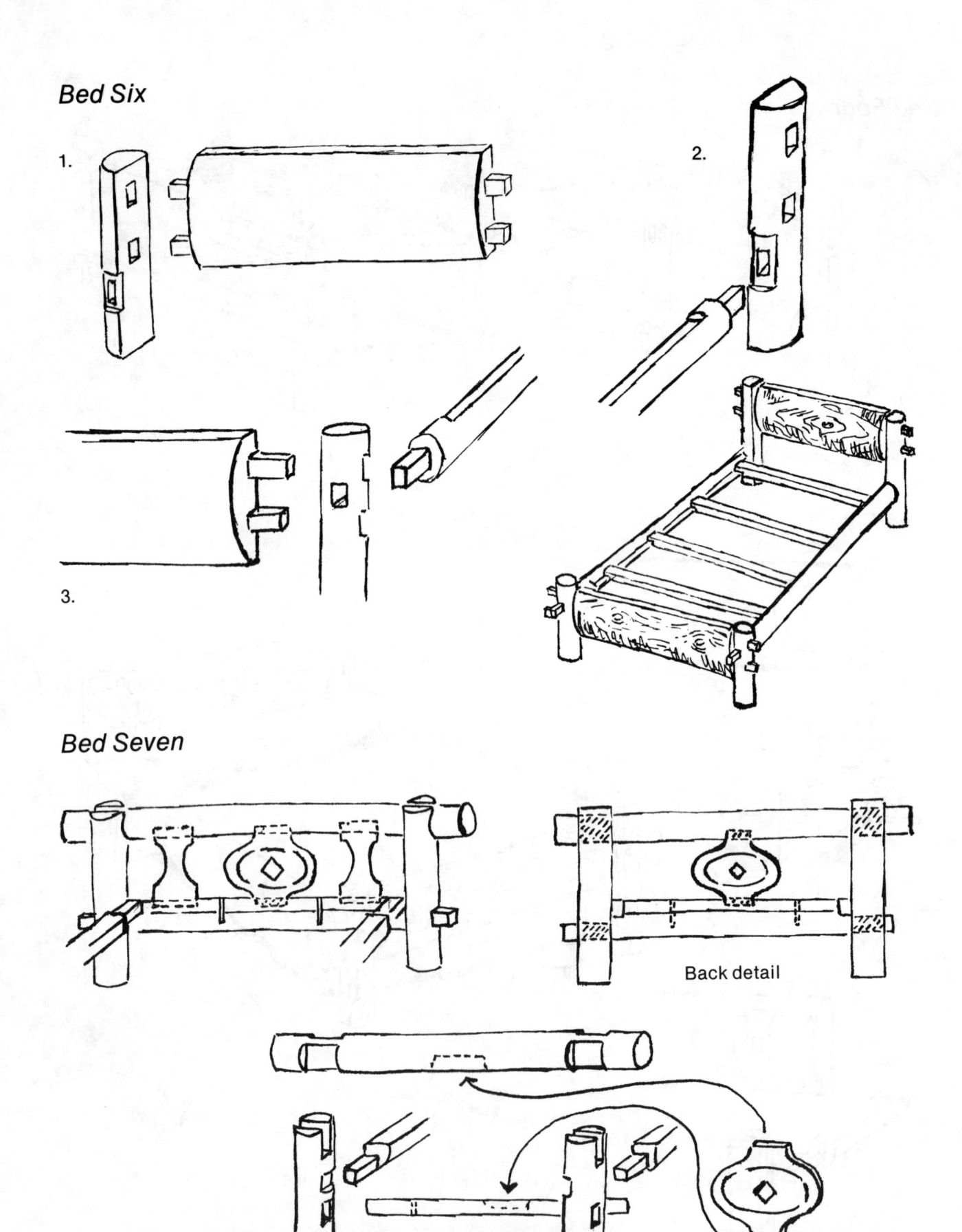

1.

2.

3.

Bed Seven

Back detail

76

Bunk Bed

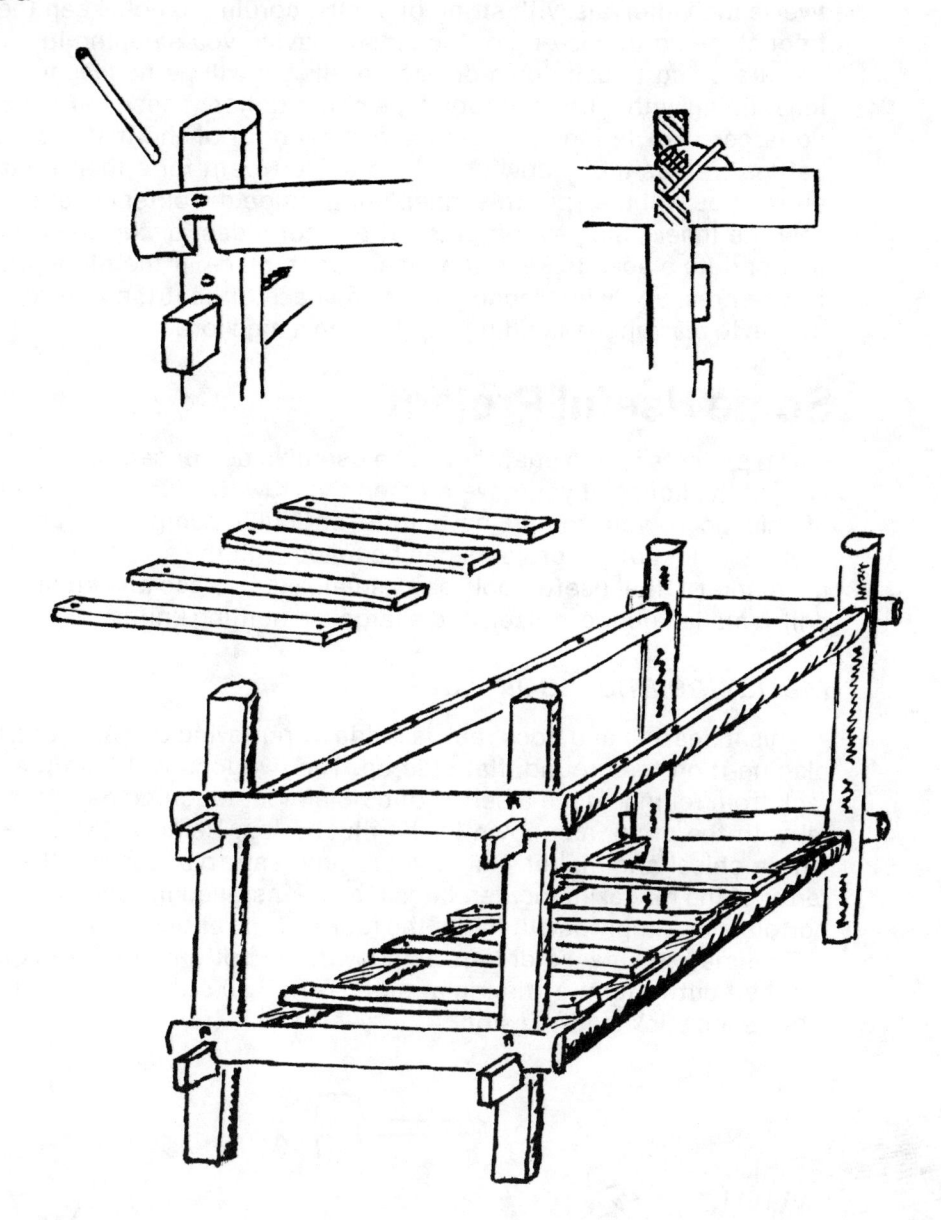

Mattresses

To make mattresses you may wish to buy large, thick sheets of foam rubber. This foam rubber works well even over hard plywood. For stuffed mattresses, you may use any type of tightly woven cloth or canvas you have available. For filling a stuffed mattress you may use soft, dead and dry pine, spruce, fir, or hemlock needles or well dried straw or hay. If you have been saving your duck and goose down, you may also use it for mattress stuffing. The filling from old down or dacron sleeping bags can also be reused.

I have found the easiest way to make an outer shell or covering for the mattress is to take two appropriate sized pieces of fabric for the top and bottom and lay them inside out, right sides together. Sew the two long ends and one short end, having a large seam allowance. Leave one end open to turn right side out. After sewing together the three sides, turn right side out. Then stuff with the desired filling, turn under the seam allowance and sew the opening. It is best at this point to tie the mattress at about six to twelve inch intervals with string or similar cording to help keep the stuffing from all going to one end or the sides, leaving you sleeping in a hollow. If you are going to use down or dacron filler, it will be necessary to sew an inner lining with baffles or tube-type construction. These baffles should be no larger than ten inches wide and the length of the mattress. Stuff the baffles with as much down or filling as you want for either a hard or soft effect. You will then put this inner lining inside the outer covering. You can sew the inner lining to the outer at all four sides, or tie them together in appropriate places to keep the inner bag in place. If the filling has shifted to one area, you will probably have to shake or beat the mattress once in awhile to rearrange the filling and to keep a high loft.

Some Useful Projects

The projects in this chapter will be useful in den or cabin, on the patio, or around the house. If you have studied the How-to section at the beginning of this book, you should have little difficulty completing any of these projects. Most of the projects can be made with the smallest chain saw on the market. Other useful tools are a small axe, a brace and bit or an electric drill, a mallet, gouge, chisel, and a large old hunting knife.

Magazine and Book Rack

This magazine and book rack is made by removing one side of a log, then placing it on the ground, flat side up. The two logs will help prevent your rack from rolling. Make a series of cuts almost touching each other, parallel with the grain, as shown in the illustration. Remove the excess wood with a chisel and mallet. Using your chain saw, plane down the rough interior of the magazine holder. Legs may be installed in several ways, or the bottom may simply be cut flat, if the rack is large enough.

To install the braces or legs as shown, the bottom of the rack has been notched out to form a triangular slot. Using two sticks for braces or legs, carve each stick to fit the slot.

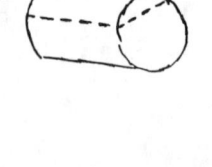

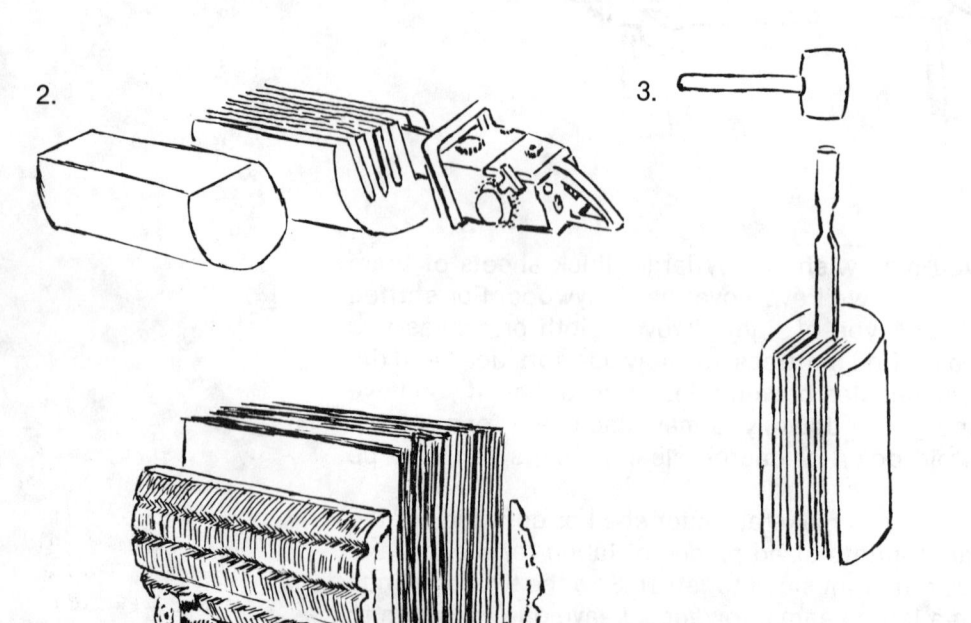

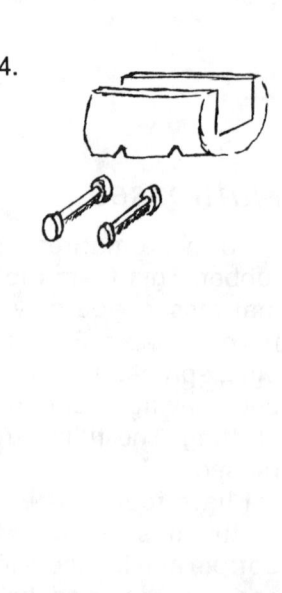

Lamps

Lamp one is made from a two piece stump or a crotch in a tree. The high side is drilled through and an eight inch length of copper pipe is then driven down four inches into the top of the lamp base. A smaller log is then drilled out in the center and fitted down over the protruding four inches of copper pipe in the base. A second eight inch length of copper pipe is driven into the top of this smaller piece. You are now ready to install your electrical fixture.

Lamp One

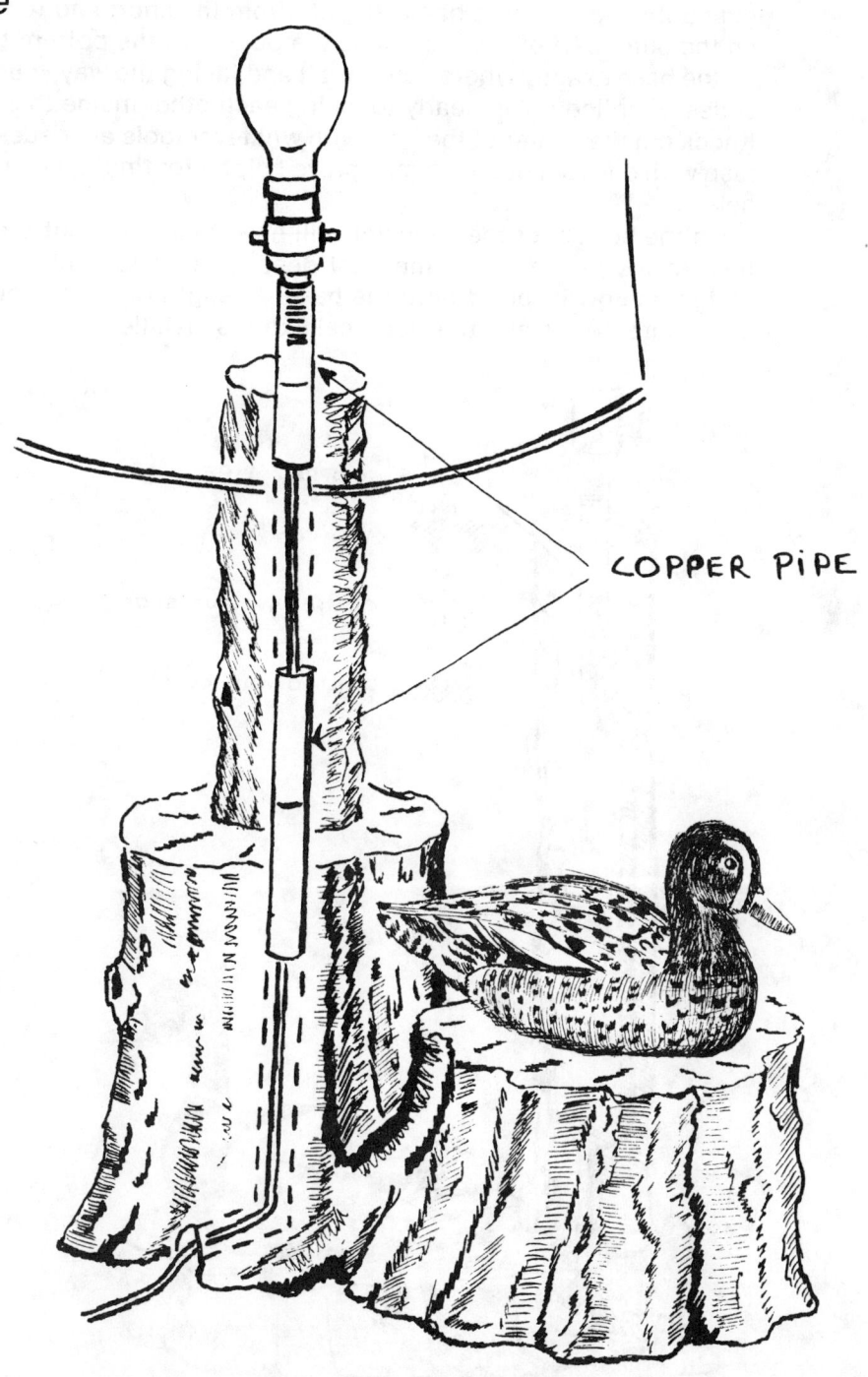

Lamp Two

Lamp two is made by cutting a wafer of hardwood from fourteen to sixteen inches in diameter and about three and one-half inches thick for the base. The height of the upright depends on whether the lamp is to be used as a floor lamp or as a table lamp. Drill out the center of this upright from both ends as deep as the length of your drill bit will allow. Now on the back side of this upright, make a plunge cut slot joining the top drill hole with the bottom one as shown in the drawing. Measure up from the bottom on the upright a distance equal to the thickness of the base, completely ringing the upright. At this point cut in about one-eighth of its diameter. With an old hunting knife and a hammer, split from the short end to the ringed cut on the outer part of the log. Trace the outline of the bottom to be inserted on the base exactly where you want it and facing the way you want. Make a series of drilled holes nearly touching each other inside this drawn circle. Knock out the center of the hole with whatever tools are necessary. A wood rasp with one rounded side may prove helpful for final touch up work in the hole.

On the bottom of the base you will have to cut a slight groove from the hole to the rear of the lamp, just deep enough to accept the cord. The upright is now inserted onto the base. A length of copper pipe should be driven into the top and the electrical fixtures installed.

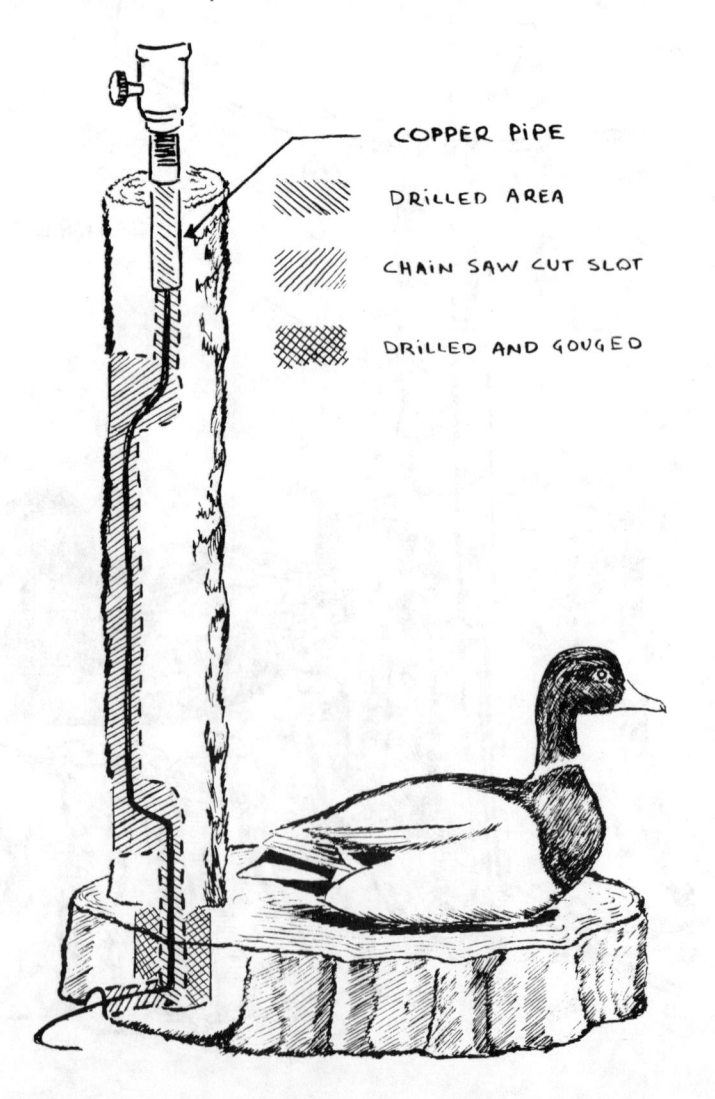

The duck decoys at the base of these two lamps can be carved in part with a small chain saw. There are instructions in the How-to section under Carving. These lamps also lend themselves well to other decorations such as shed antlers, potted plants, dry flower arrangements, ash trays, old spurs and other rusted iron.

Plaques

Plaques are made by cutting a sound log into angular wafers about one inch thick on about a forty-five degree angle. It is best to use your smallest chain saw with the smallest diameter chain so that there will be few, if any, chain marks left on the plaques.

There are numerous uses for these plaques. You can use them to mount antlers or horns. You can glue pictures on them, paint pictures on them, or use them for coasters.

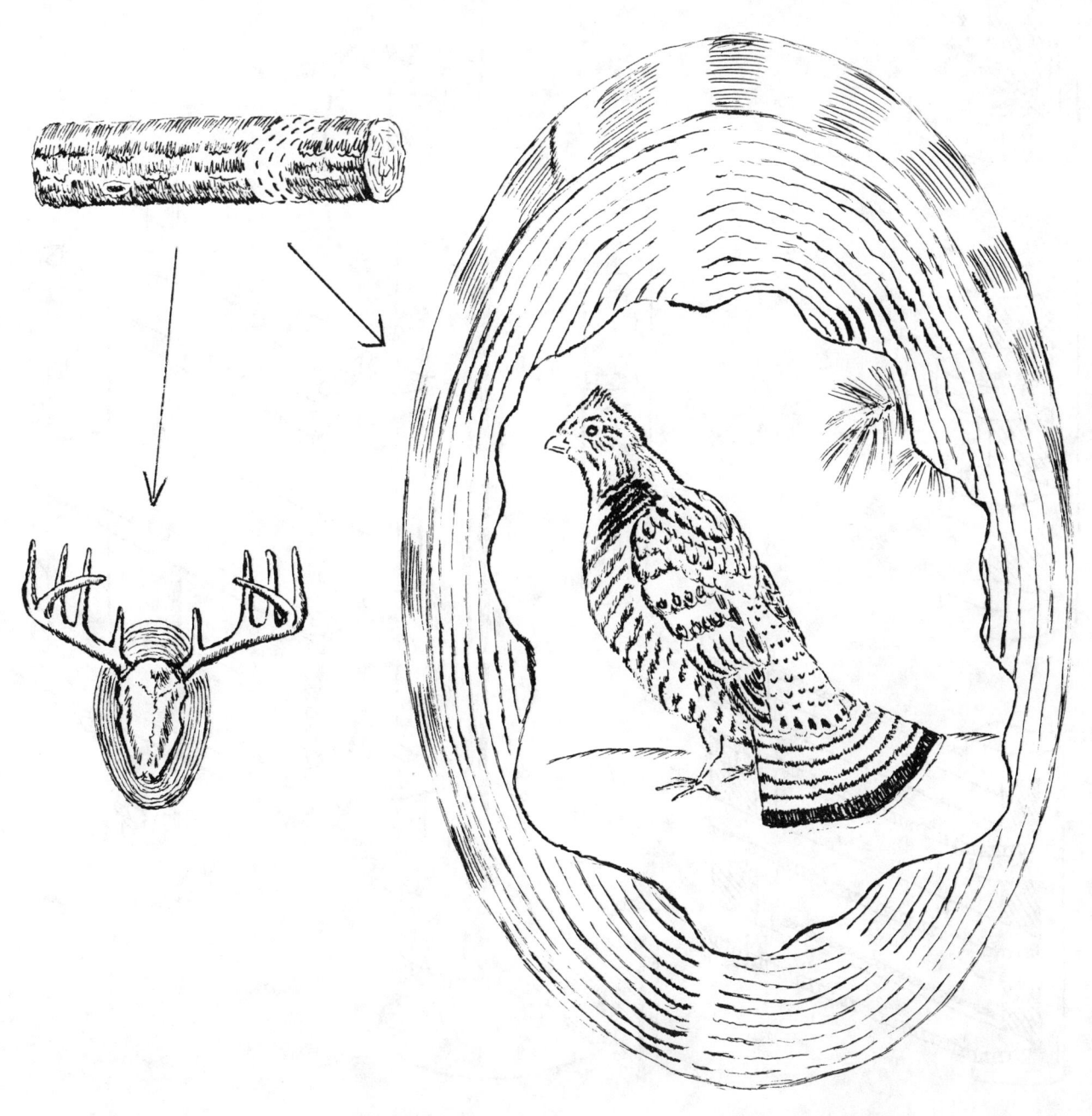

81

Shelves

The shelves illustrated here are only a few of the many methods you can use to make shelves with your chain saw. The shelves shown in the bottom drawing are made by using two of the shelves illustrated at the top right of the page. When being used as shelf supports, they must be made to face in opposite directions or inwards.

Shelves can often be made by using some of your leftover slabs from sides of logs that you have squared or those you have flattened on one side. Sometimes, by drilling holes in these slabs, you can insert rope or chain through the holes. By tying knots in the rope or inserting pegs in the chain under each shelf, you can make quite a nice shelf. For more stability you can notch out two half round upright logs and install them behind the shelves and drive the shelves into the notches of these uprights.

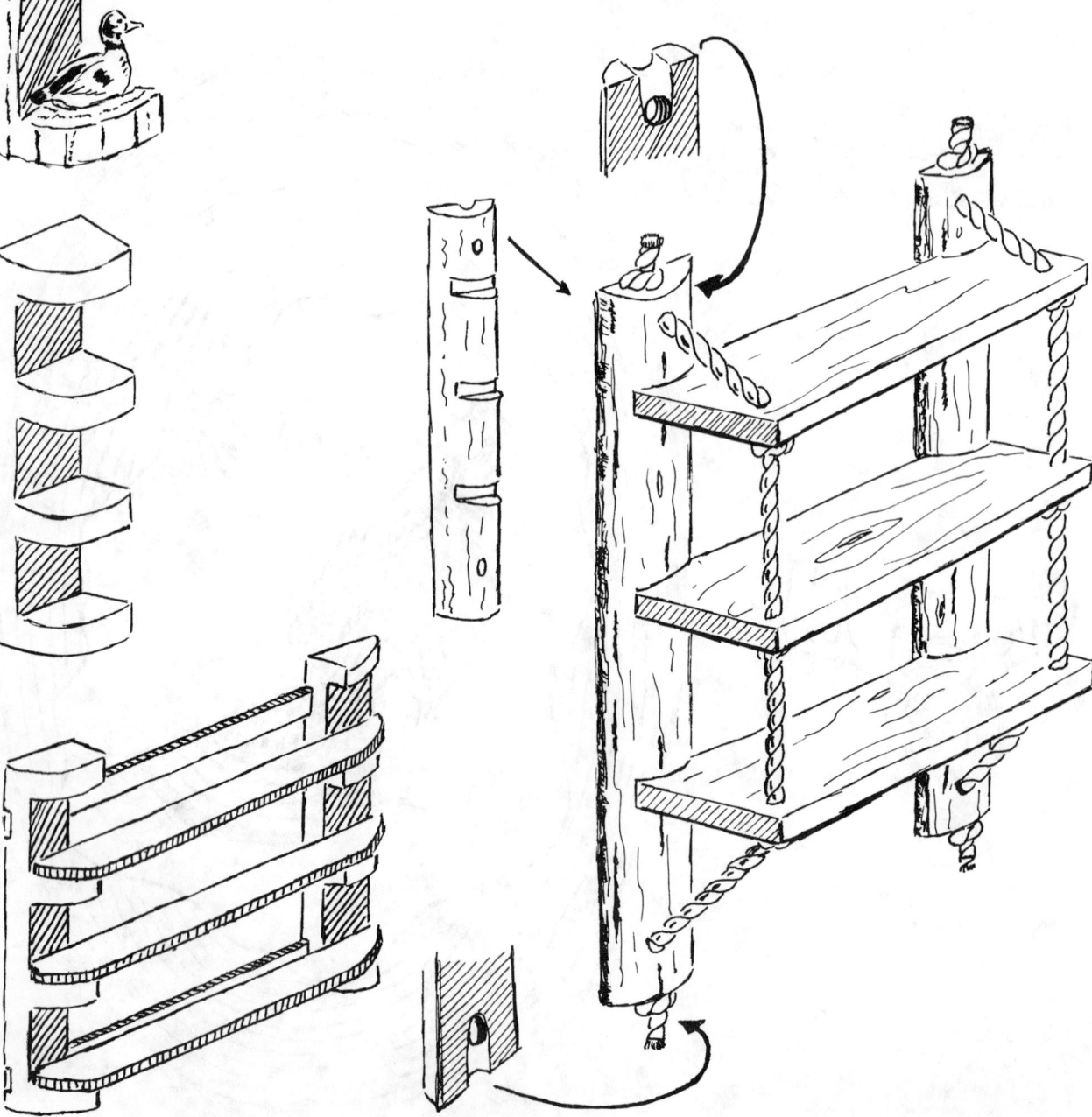

Hollow Log Items

Hollow log picture frames, arrow holders, winter flower vases or pots and fireplace wood holders are only a few of the items you can make out of hollow logs. There are numerous ways to obtain and make hollow logs. Apple wood is my favorite because it has so much character. Generally it is not difficult to find an abandoned orchard that needs a few dead trees removed or at least some of the large dead leaders removed. Most of the time it is quite easy to make some sort of a trade with the landowner. Many hollow oaks and maples also work well.

I have never found a hollow log ready to use, so I cut off one end and clean out the inside to suit my taste, removing any decay or insects. I then cut the piece I am going to use free from the main part of the log. The arrow holder is simply a cleaned out hollow log glued or pegged to a wafer about an inch larger in diameter. The flower vase or pot is made in a similar manner. Sometimes you will find that you have small wafers or chunks of firewood lying around that seem to have too much character to burn or throw away. These can be made into picture frames or plaques. To hollow out these thin pieces for picture frames, use a power drill, or a brace and bit. Drill holes almost touching one another on the inside perimeter of the frame. Drill numerous holes at one end to prevent cracking the frame when you remove the center with a gouge and mallet. These extra holes will make room for the wood being displaced by the gouge.

The firewood holder's main body may be made in various ways. One method is by removing one-quarter to one-third from one side of a hollow log. Another method is to cut off one side of a solid log and make numerous rip cuts from the flat side down. See the illustration for the magazine holder or the cradle in the chapter on toys. Legs may be inserted pegs or glued on blocks.

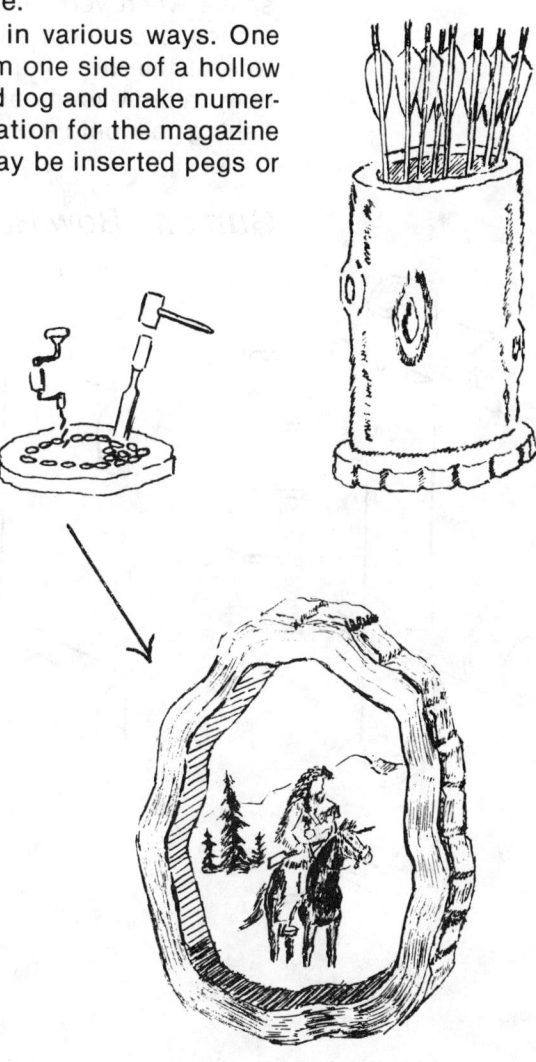

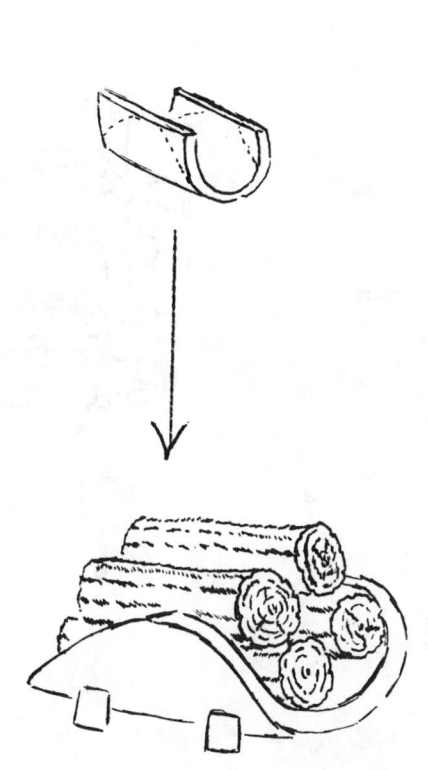

Gun and Bow Cabinets and Racks

These gun and bow cabinets and racks are but a few of the many styles and plans you can use in making similar cabinets and racks with your chain saw and a few other small hand tools.

It is far better to design the cabinet or rack that best suits your purpose. The amount of room you have in your den or cabin, the number of rifles, shotguns, handguns, bows, fishing rods, etc., are some of the more important factors to consider when designing a gun and/or bow cabinet or rack.

The combination gun and bow cabinet that I have illustrated was designed to fit my longest bow and my longest shotgun. The notched piece was set high enough for the longest forearm of my Model 70, which also happens to be short enough for my Model 94 and my Ithaca 22 lever action. I wanted to have a four inch magazine rack under the bottom of the cabinet; however the ceiling of the house I lived in at the time would not allow both the magazine rack on the bottom and the fox mount on top. I needed a place for my fox more than I needed a magazine rack, so I chose the one over the other. I prefer to have handguns either in the bedroom of a suburban home, or in the kitchen of a cabin where most of your indoor, daylight hours are spent. Fishing poles can be hung vertically on hooks, and quite closely together to stay safe and clean, and not take up otherwise needed space. Generally speaking, rifles and shotguns take up less wall space when vertical than when horizontal. There are exceptions, for instance, over doors and archways, windows, mantels, and bunk beds, etc. One of the most important things to remember in building your gun and bow cabinet, is to carefully consider and measure all of your hunting and fishing gear before drawing up your plans.

Gun and Bow Rack

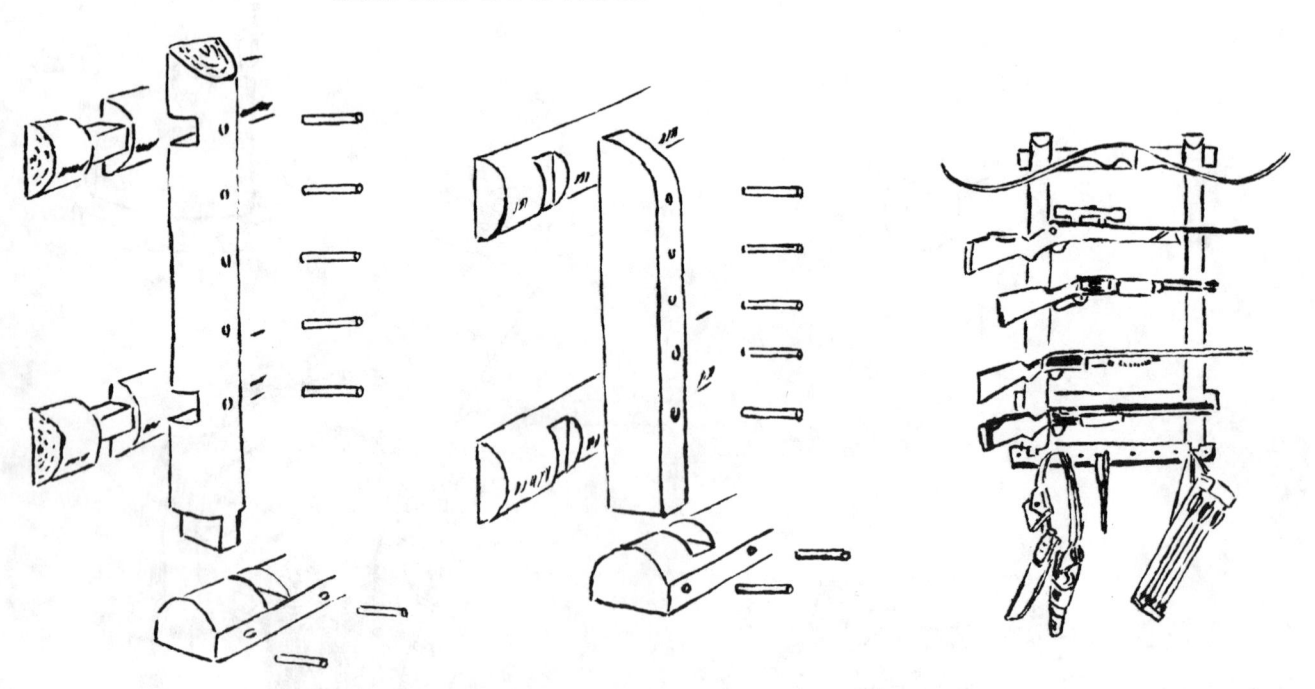

Gun and Bow Cabinet

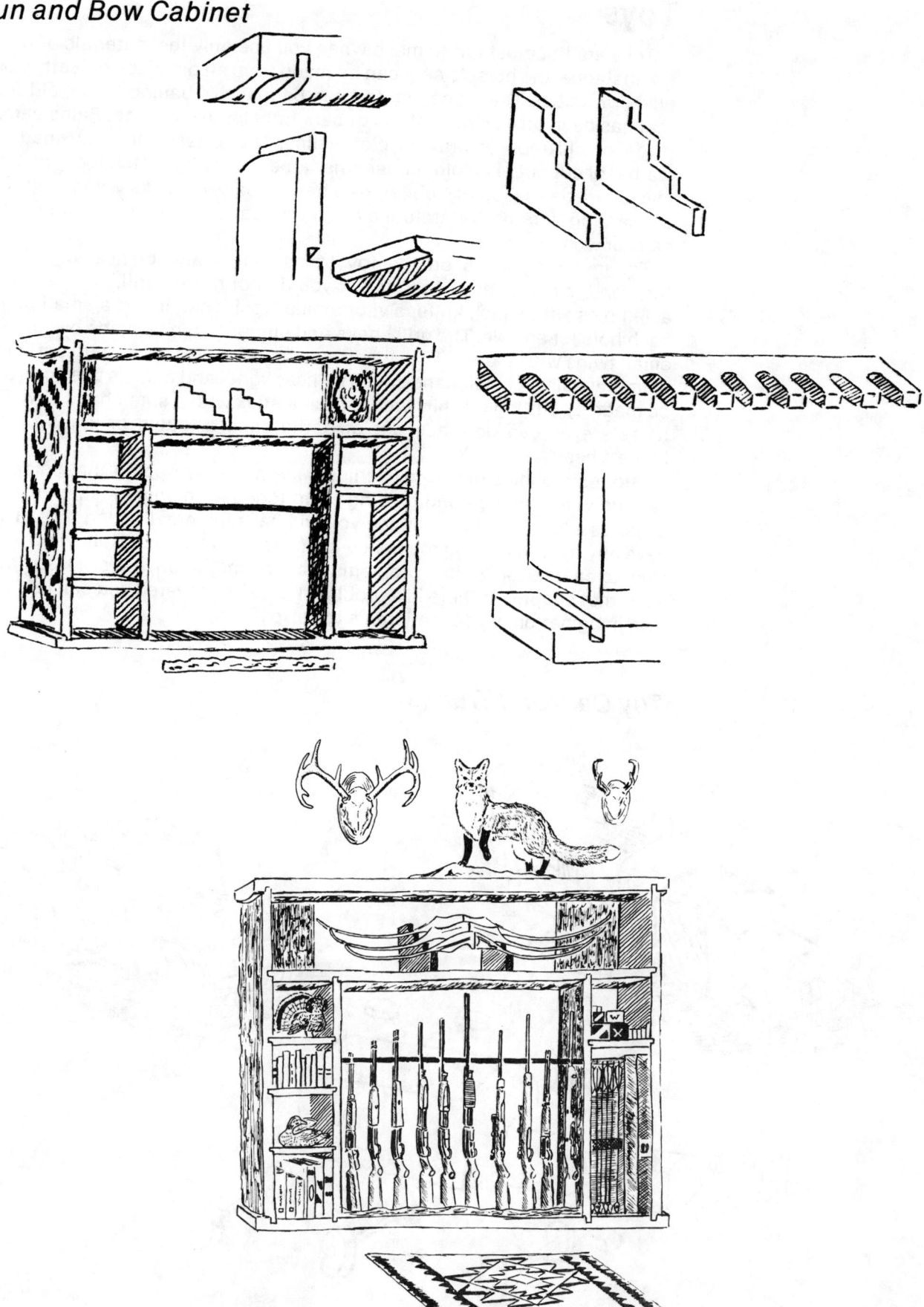

85

Toys

Toys are the most fun to make when you use only the materials at hand. For instance, the horse's ears can be made from an old piece of leather or a piece of rubber. The mane and tail can be made of bailing twine, old rope that has been unwoven, or strips of bark from large old vines. Reins can be made of old rope or braided clothesline. Drum heads may be made of leather or cut out of an old rubber inner tube. The cattle catcher on the train may be made of leather, rubber, tree bark or carved from a wood chip. The connecting bars on the train may join one car to another by using small nails or wooden pegs.

For installing axles on the toy trains, autos and planes, drill holes through the main body of the toy. If you do not have a drill, you can make axle holes with a jack knife, awl or similar tool. Then insert a small peg in each hole for an axle. The grill shells and bumpers can be made by splitting small twigs with a knife. The wheels can be cut out of sticks with sufficient diameter using a small hand saw. The headlights and horse's eyes can also be made by cutting off thin wafers from a stick with a small hand saw. The horse's eyes can be made out of bottle caps or stubs of limbs on the horse's head.

The main bodies of the toy vehicles are made by ripping three sides of various diameter logs and glueing them together in some fashion that resembles a known vehicle. I hope you will have fun creating log toys. If you have any trouble making the hollow drum, refer to Through Hollowing in the How-to chapter. Any other problems that you might run into are also covered in that chapter. If there is a problem I have not covered you can use your own imagination or your children's to solve it.

Toy Cars and Trucks

Toy Train

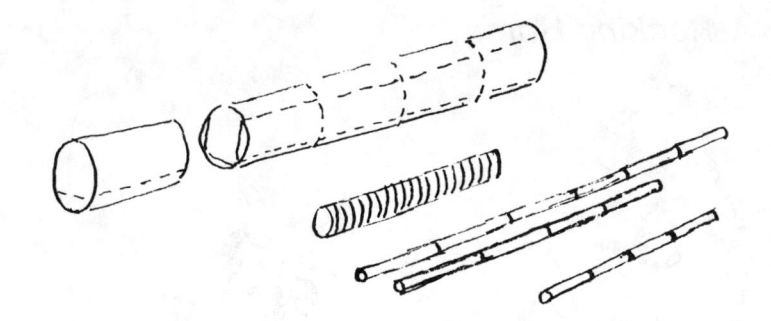

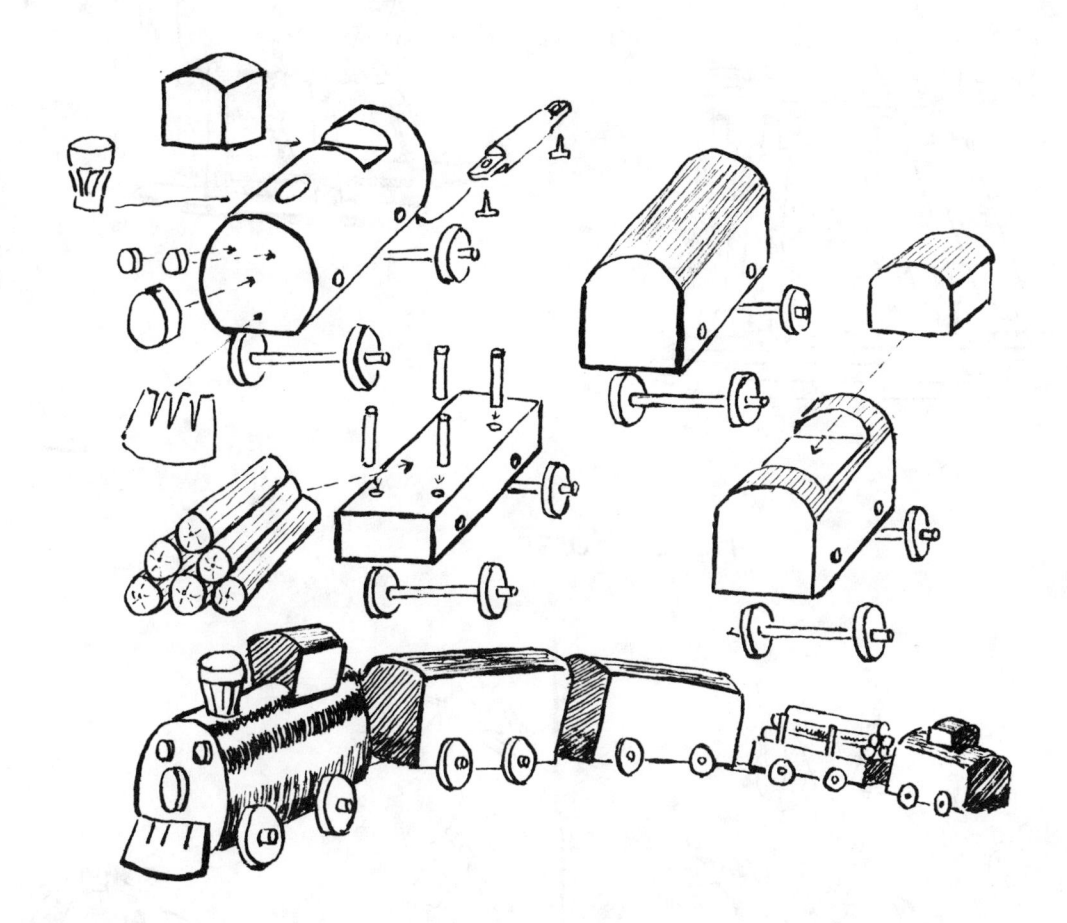

Toy Airplane

87

Rocking Horse

Hobby Horse

88

Toy Cradle

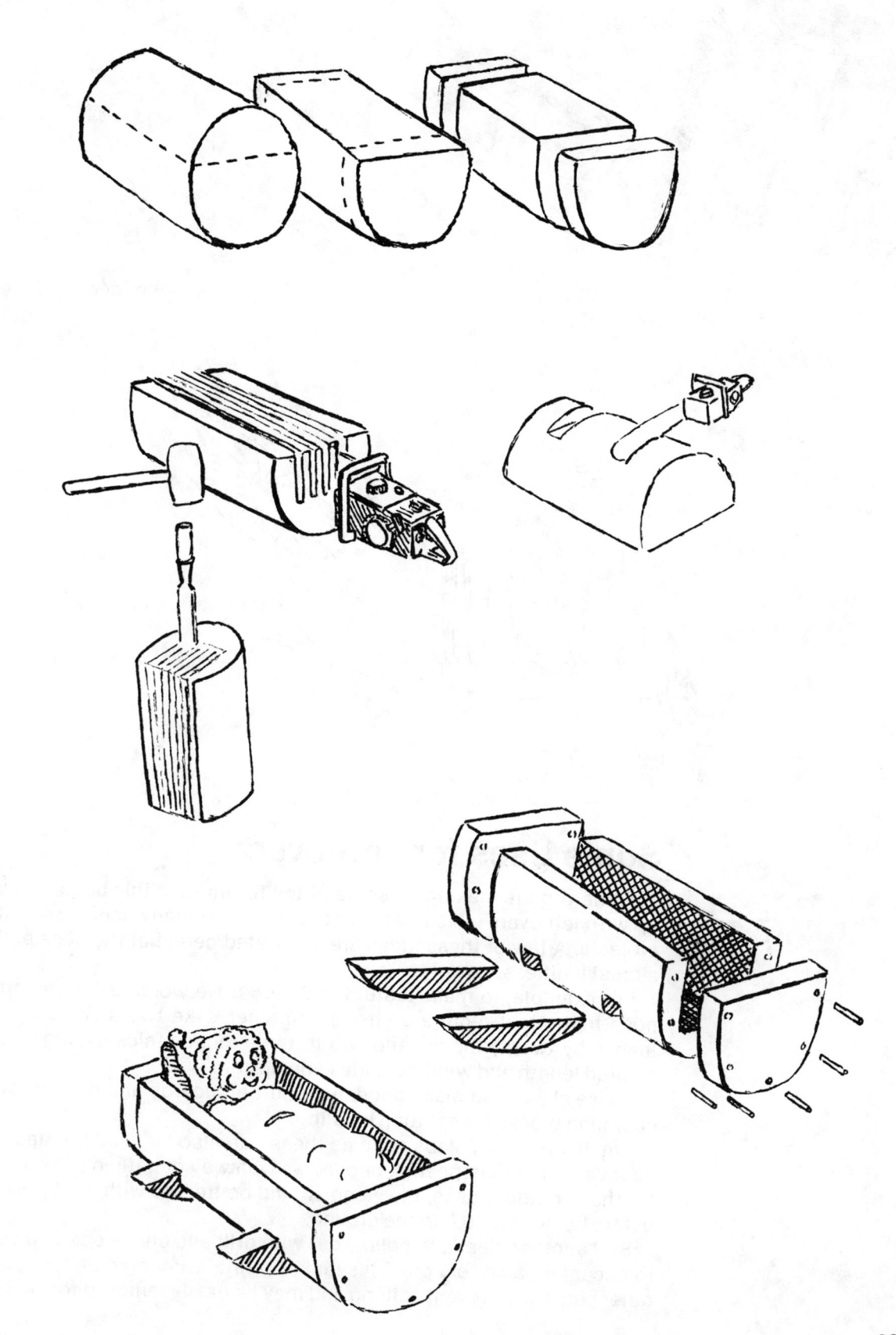

Toy Indian Drum
(Made of Hollow Logs)

Leather or rubber innertube

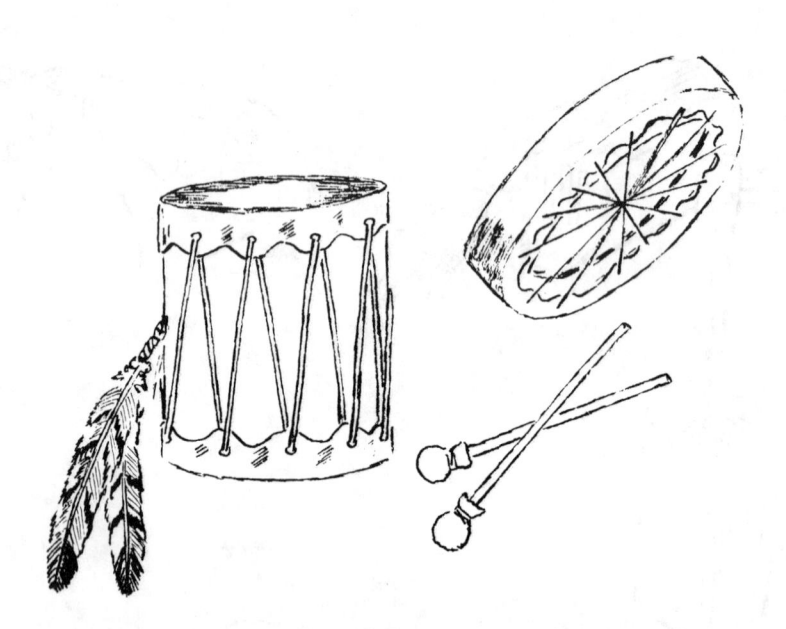

Some Uses for Left-overs

While you are making up some of the furniture in this book, you will end up with left-overs which can be converted into many useful and attractive projects. A few of these ideas are illustrated here, but the possibilities are almost limitless.

For example, to make a sturdy box for stove wood or for any other purpose that might require a strong container, take two slabs about twenty inches by twenty inches and two to three inches thick. Nail on boards of desired length and width for sides and bottom.

These slabs also make good meat cutting boards and butcher blocks or chopping blocks for splitting kindling.

Small, imperfect slabs such as these can also be used for steps around your yard or summer camp, or used as walkway or patio blocks. Of course, for these outdoor uses, the wood should be treated with a rot preventative before being placed into the ground.

Still another idea is to hollow out with drill and chisel one of these slabs to accept a pail or old pot. This makes a fine watering dish for your dog or other pet. It will prevent spilling and may be easily removed for cleaning.

Posts

Bookholder

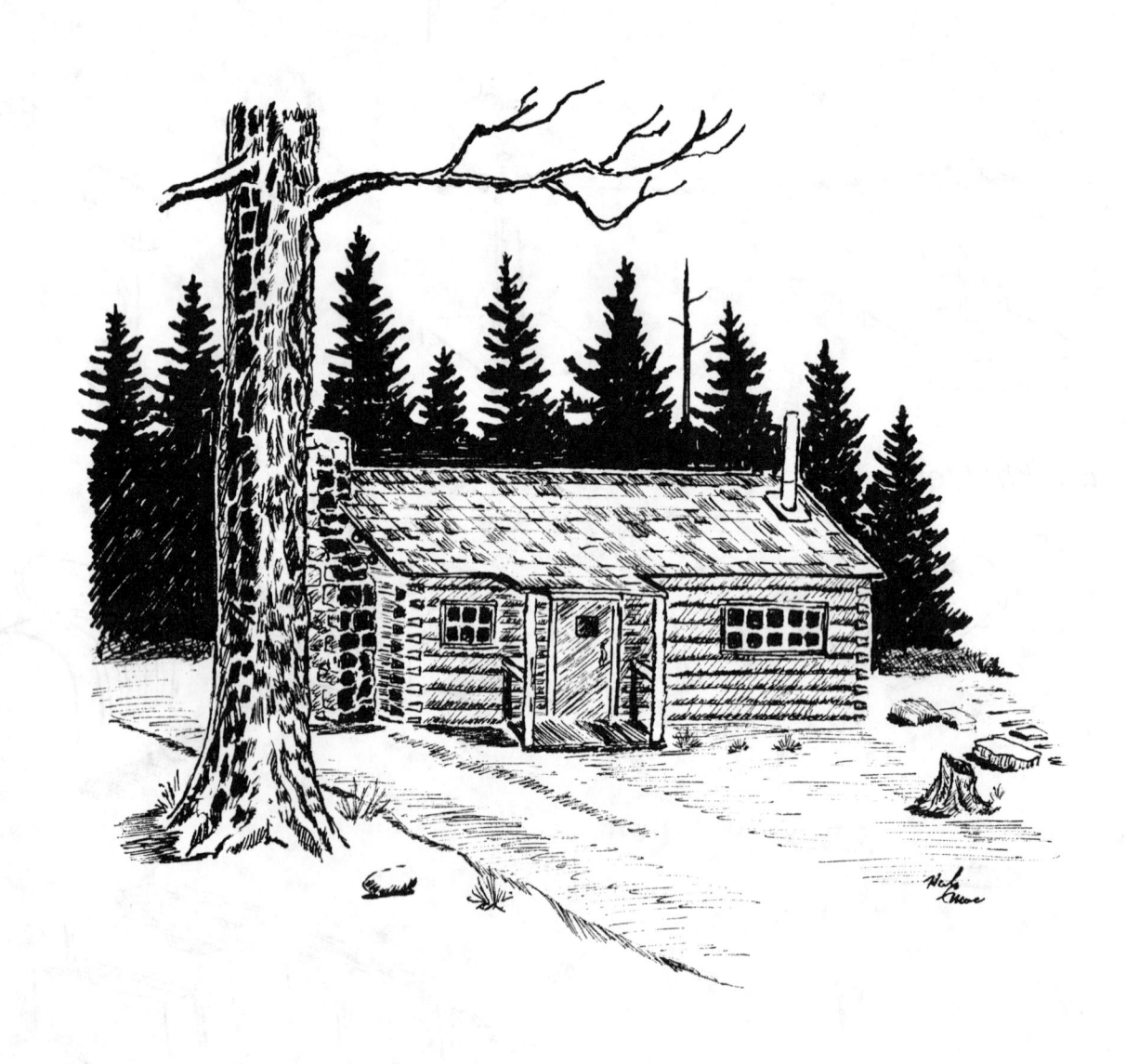

6.
Log Structures

Log cabin building has been going on in this country since the first white man set foot on the continent. Many of the cabin craftsmen from the Old World brought their skills of fine log structure craftsmanship with them. Other men obviously without these skills had to invent or create methods of building log shelters to suit their needs and the needs of their particular environment. The tools they had to work with and the time they had to build the necessary construction for winter also played a major role in the type of log construction they used.

The reason that I have mentioned the above is to assure you that I am not going to try to give you any new, improved ideas for building log structures. I will, however, attempt to give you a few pointers on how to, with the aid of your chain saw, cut your construction time down to a fraction of that of the old timers with their axes and hand saws.

As I write this chapter, I am quite fortunate to be spending my second winter in a cabin in the mountains of southwestern Colorado. In this mountain valley there are cabins built with every conceivable type of construction a person can imagine. Some of these cabins are over one hundred years old. Some are still lived in year round. Others are old mining cabins that were and are only accessible on horseback or on foot. Some of the old ranches that had houses and barns built out of logs are still intact. However, the old ranch roads have been obliterated by new forests since the ranches have been abandoned.

Wintering in a tight cabin is quite enjoyable, wintering in a rail corral is almost impossible. All of your time is wasted trying to keep warm and dry. Then after trying to keep warm and dry all winter, you have to keep out the insects in the spring and summer. The thing I am trying to get across here is that it is better to build a solid, really tight cabin when you first build than it is to waste the rest of your life trying to keep comfortable in a sloppily fitted cabin.

In this chapter on structures, I have illustrated only six of the methods of linking cabins together. These methods are quite primitive but also very efficient. If you have made much of the furniture in this book, you will have few problems building a cabin if you can obtain the logs for the structure.

Types of Log Joints

Types of Dovetail Joints

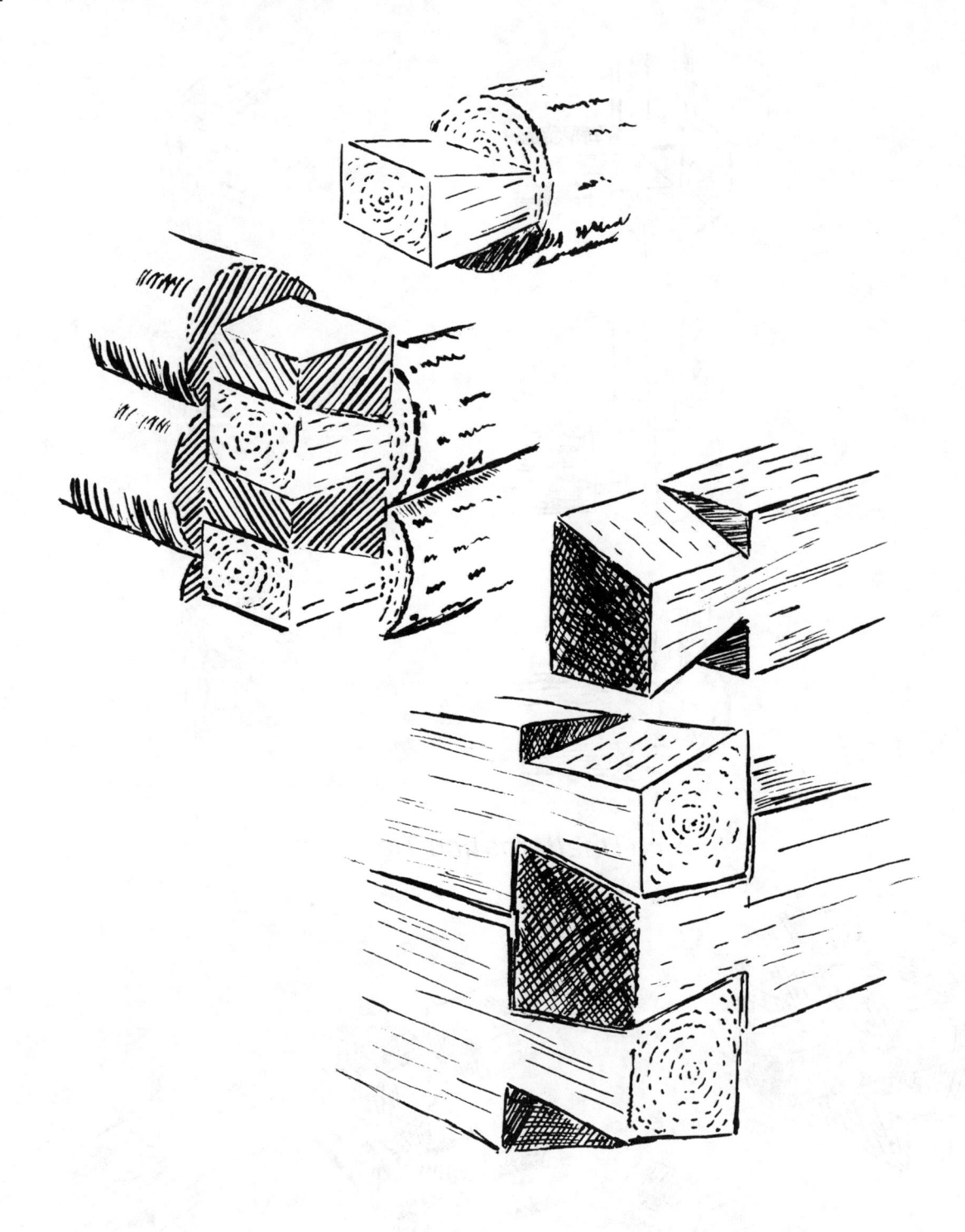

Corner Posts

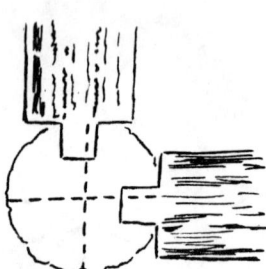

1.
2.
3.

Joining Unalternating Tiers

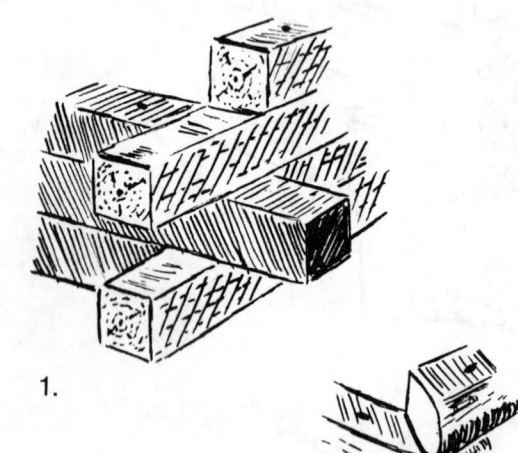

1.
2. 
3.
4.

One Type of Prebuilt Wall

Use upright or horizontal

Corner Post

Stairs and Ladders

Foundations

Foundation building will depend greatly on the use you plan to give your cabin, the number of years you want it to last and the weather conditions in which you live. In southwestern Colorado, there are many cabins over one hundred years old which are built on simply laid walls of dry stone. More frequently than not these walls are just high enough on all four sides to make a level footing to start building the cabin. My mountain valley, although high in elevation, does not get as much wet snow or rain as the northeast or the northwest. A few cabins in this valley are built on log skids just in case one wishes a slight change of scenery.

I believe that the minimum foundation anyone should use is creosote treated upright pillars. Better pillars can be made of poured concrete and stone using a cardboard cylinder for the form or mold. The twenty-five gallon or fifty gallon oil barrels also make fine molds or forms.

For log cabins, stone foundations, whether dry wall or cemented, seem to be the most appealing and the cheapest to build providing the stones are readily available.

Farm structures, however, which might come into heavy abuse by a discontented bull or a hot-rod tractor driver, will last longer if you use metal drums full of concrete and rock, using steel plates built into them for bolting onto your main floor joists.

If you are planning to build either a full basement foundation or a concrete slab and if you are not a professional builder in the area where the cabin is to be built, I suggest you check with your local building code officer. If there is no officer available, check with your local builders to find out which type of full basement foundation or concrete slab is best suited for the area where you are building your cabin.

Cabin Deck Construction

The process of joining the cabin deck to the walls will be one of the deciding factors on how warm and critter-proof the completed cabin will be.

If you are going to use milled lumber for the framing and cross members of the deck and your walls are to be built of round logs, You will want to take your chain saw and rip off the rounded inside of the logs for that tier to which the milled lumber, deck framing will be nailed.

When using logs for cross members of a deck, it is easiest to first build your cabin wall up one or two tiers. Rip with your chain saw each cross member on the one side to be used facing up, to which your sub-flooring will be nailed. Square off the ends of your measured deck stringers. Notch the wall logs to accept the squared ends of the deck stringers. The next tier of logs for the cabin wall should be ripped flat on the inward side before being set in place. These flat, inward logs will be easier to work with when laying down a tightly fitted sub-flooring and additional flooring.

Doors and Windows

Frequently, when building small cabins and other small log structures, it is easier and more expedient to build the cabin's four walls with full length logs. Then after the walls are up and the cross braces installed, measure your doors and windows including sills and framing. Mark out the area of logs to be removed, spike or nail planks on the outside of the vertical marks flush with the drawn lines. These upright spiked planks will keep your cabin intact and prevent saw pinching while you are cutting out and removing the door and window openings. The next step is to install the permanent window and door framing using stout planking and nails or spikes of sufficient size. To prevent damage to windows and doors, it is best not to install them until the roof is completed and most of the interior work is done. The most convenient time to remove the temporary bracing around the door and window openings is when you are ready to install the doors and windows; however if you are going to chink the cabin before you install the doors and windows, this is the time to remove the temporary bracing.

Roof Construction

There are three basic types of roof designs used in log structure building. You will find all three types illustrated on the following pages.

The first type is the *linked-lock log type*. This is perhaps the strongest type of roof. It is best suited to heavy snow country when used to build a small cabin. This type of construction is found most frequently in the remotest parts of the country.

The second type employs the use of a main, *single ridge pole* and the side roof rafters are secured to it and to the top plate of the structure.

The third type of roof rafter design employs the use of a *pre-built truss.* An appropriate number of these trusses can be made either up on the top deck of the structure or, if you have a derrick or crane of sorts, you can make them on the ground and lift them up onto the top deck. These trusses are generally set in place and temporarily braced until the cross roofing is employed to hold them permanently.

The pitch at which you design your roof should depend on how close the rafters will be to each other, the diameter of the rafters, the thickness and strength of the roofing boards. Most trappers' and miners' cabins in heavy snow country that I have seen, have shallowly pitched roofs, but employ the use of very stout roof beams which withstand the heavy weight of the snow. Many of the more recently constructed cabins have very steeply pitched roofs with many very thin rafters.

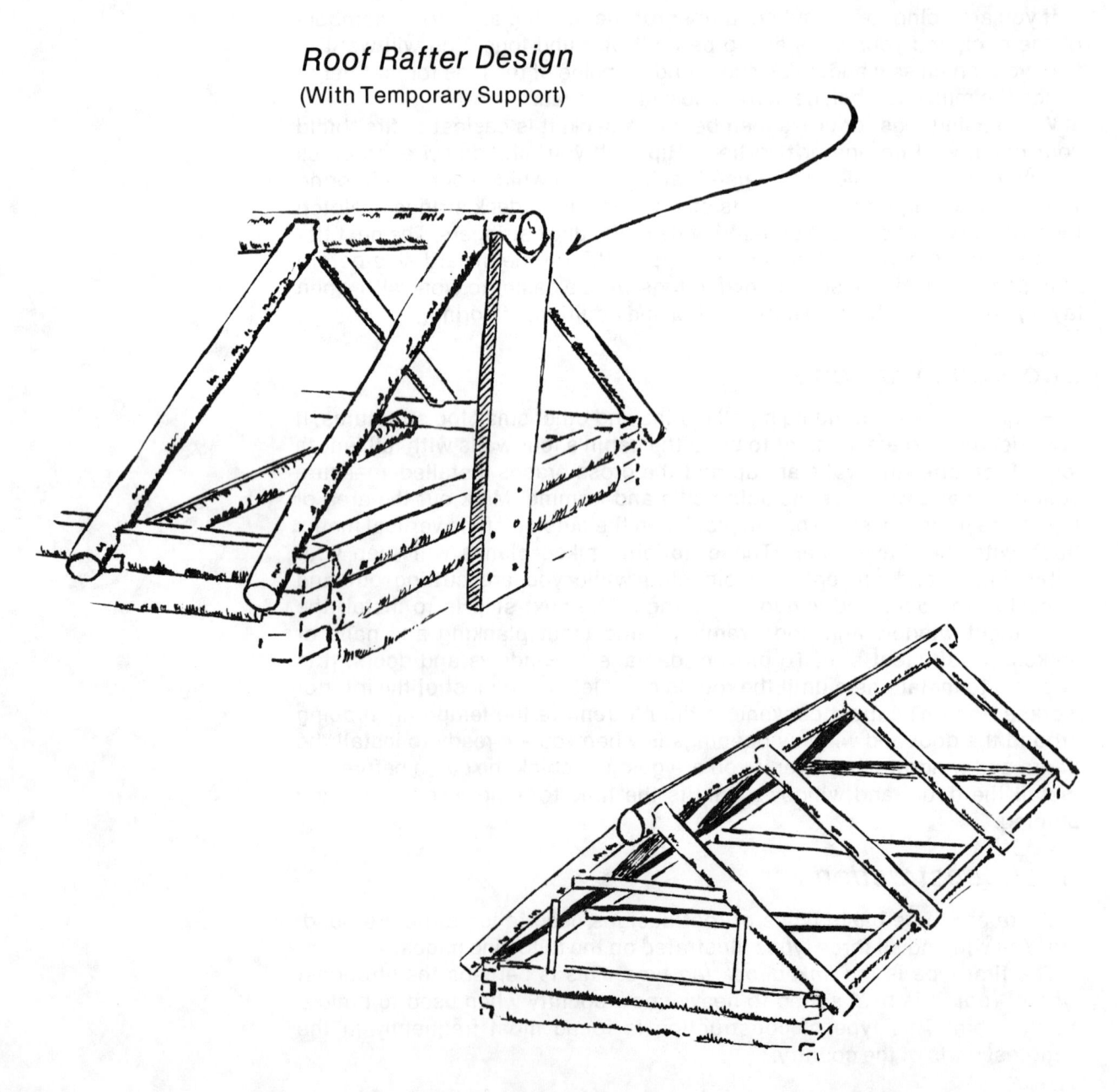

Roof Rafter Design
(With Temporary Support)

Roof Rafters—Linked Locked Log Design

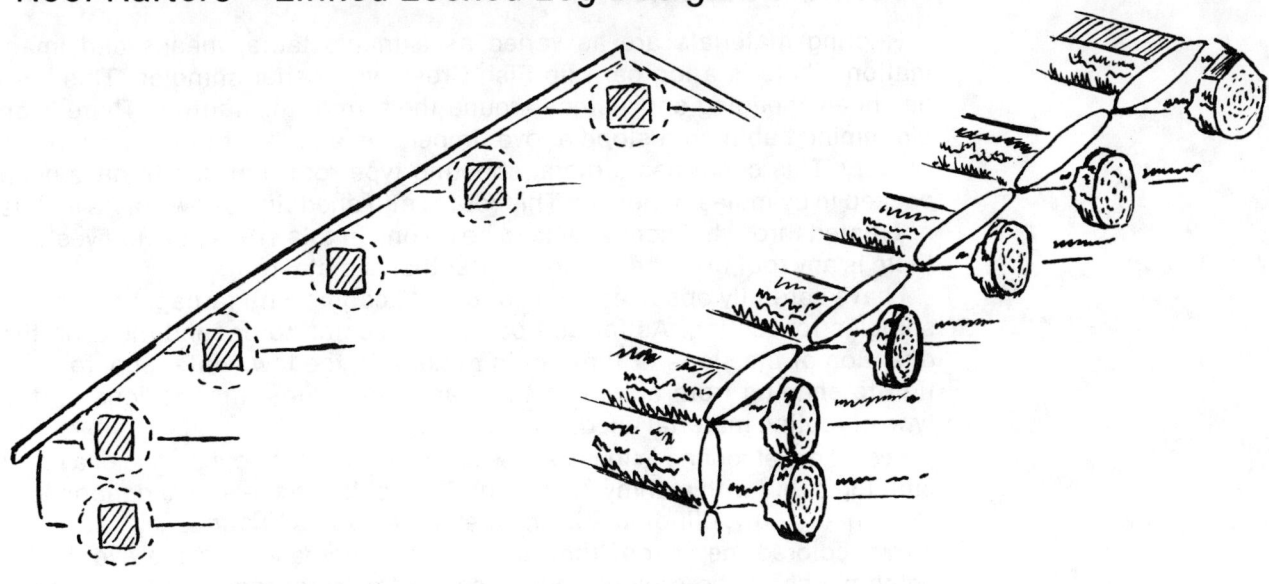

Roof Truss Design

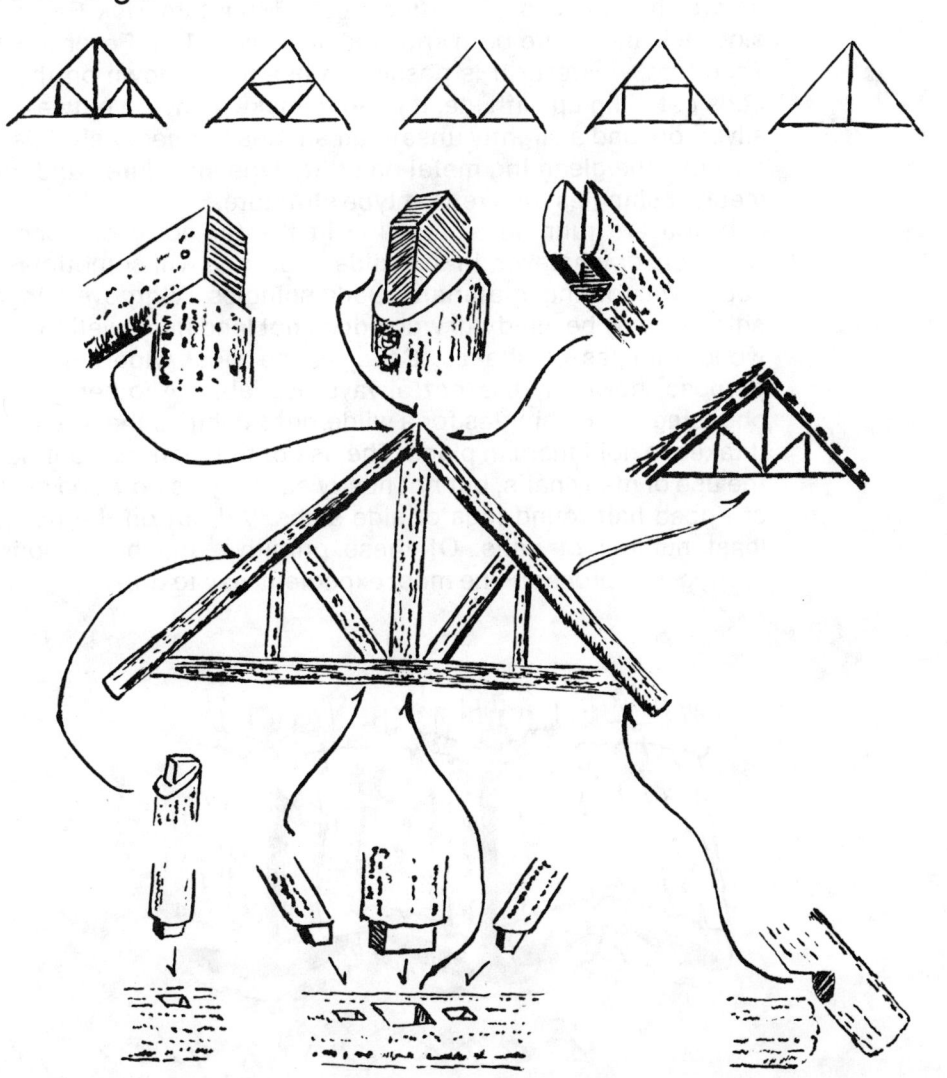

Roofing Materials

Roofing materials are as varied as a man's taste, means and imagination. There is a log barn up Fish Creek with cedar shingles. This barn has been shedding snow since around the turn of the century. There is an old mining cabin on a slope above timber line also built at the turn of the century. This cabin has a metal sheeting type roof that had to have been packed in by mules or horses. This roof is still shedding snow wherever it is not rusted through. There seems to be no one in this area who believes that there is any roof that sheds snow better than a metal roof.

I have carefully observed some of the old cabins with tarpaper and cedar shingles for roofing. As far as I can tell, it seems to depend more on the direction of the slope of the roof in relation to the low winter sun, in addition to shading from adjoining trees and mountains, than it does on the type of roofing material used.

Even if metal roofing is the best, I would never ruin the appearance of a finely built log cabin with a shiny silver roof. They shine in the sun and moonlight like a giant, ugly, blinding mirror. One of the cabins in our valley has a dull brown colored metal roof that is not at all unpleasing to the eye. In my opinion, one of the greatest advantages of a metal roof is that you don't have to worry about a hot spark from your chimney landing on dry cedar or tarpaper shingles. The chances of such a disaster may be very slight, but so are the chances of getting Rocky Mountain Tick Fever. However, my side kick and I were both knocked down with Tick Fever this past summer. Therefore, wherever it is possible, I like to cut down on the chance of the odds catching up with me. If I had to make a choice between an ugly, safe, silver roof and a slightly unsafe tar shingled or cedar shingled roof, I would only use the gleaming metal on utility type structures and choose painted metal or shingles for a retreat type structure.

If you are running a trap line in the far north or conducting wildlife research, or whatever, in the wilderness, you will sometimes have to make your own roofing materials. Bark shingles, V-grooved logs, or wooden shingles may be used. All wood does not lend itself well to being made into wood shingles or shakes. Cedar is the most widely used wood for this purpose; however it is not always available. Another great drawback in choosing wood shingles for a wilderness cabin is the great number of nails it takes to hold them in place. The use of tree bark for roofing also employs the use of many nails, but not nearly as many as do wood shingles. The use of ripped half round logs or side slabs, V'd out on the flat side, uses the least number of nails. Of these primitive and backwoods methods of roofing, it is probably the most expedient way to go.

Bark Shingles

Riped half round and V-grooved

Run full length

Side slabs V-grooved

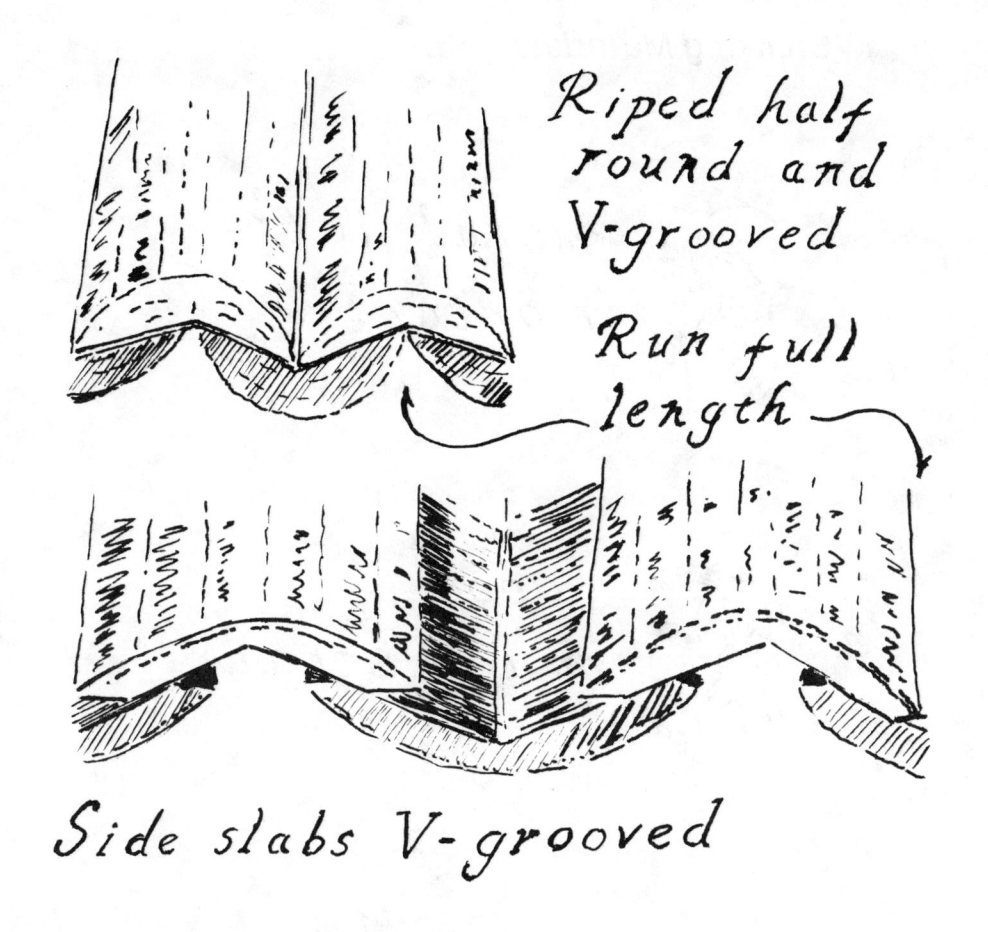

Chinking of Log Structures

Given what I have seen of different types and styles of chinking, I would almost rather leave the subject unattended. However, I will attempt to give you a few ideas.

Perhaps the tightest and warmest cabin in this valley is a dovetailed notch type made by some Swedes at the turn of the century. The cracks between the logs are so slight that they are merely filled with old blue jeans. My cabin is chinked with a wire screening strip the length of the logs and filled with a mixture of sandcrete and zonolite. The cabin at the south end of the ranch has quarter-round chinking blocks of wood nailed in the cracks on the inside and the cracks on the outside are filled with a mixture of mud and straw. This works well except that it needs yearly repairs. Most of the older cabins in the valley, with the exception of the finely crafted Swedish ones, have quarter-round blocks nailed on the inside cracks between the logs. The outside cracks are filled with everything from old rope, mud, rags, to steel and concrete of many and varied recipes. Moss is sometimes used in some areas, as is bark. In this area neither bark nor moss are of sufficient quality to use for chinking. The man who built the club house of the sportsmen's club to which I once belonged, made a groove about one and one-half inches deep on the top and bottom of each log, one at a time and inserted a narrow board the full length of the groove on the top of the bottom log. Then he installed the next grooved log over the top of the narrow board. This operation takes a lot of patience and a good amount of ambition, not to mention a pinch of skill. It works similar to tongue and groove lumber.

Chinking Materials

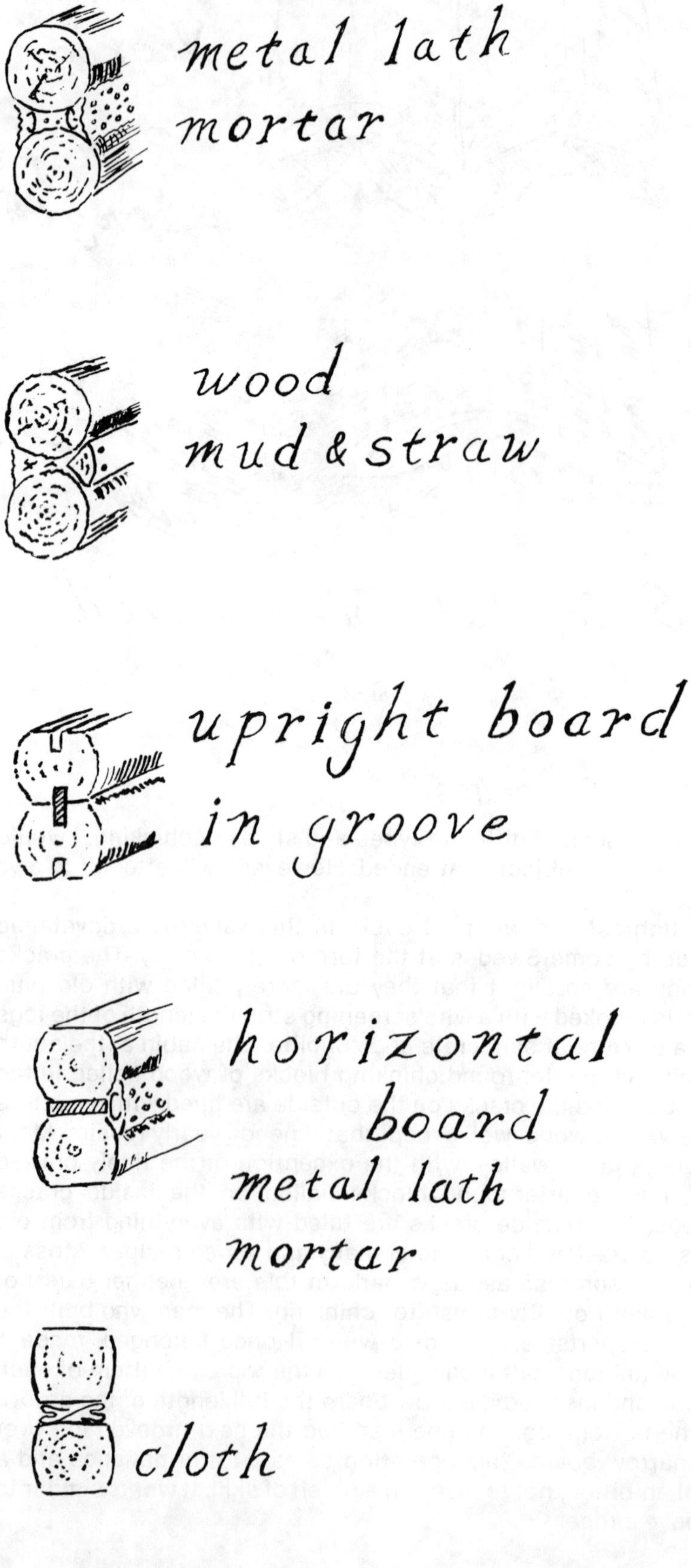

- metal lath mortar
- wood mud & straw
- upright board in groove
- horizontal board metal lath mortar
- cloth

Cabin Construction

Photos 1 and 2 show, already in place for both cabin and porch, the foundation piers of laid stone. They are laid on top of 4 feet of concrete which is under ground. Note sill logs extended out for porch deck. During construction of this cabin the entire sub floor was laid right after the sill logs were installed. This was done to give the workmen more elevation when lifting the wall logs by hand.

Photos 3 and 4 show the cabin wall built up to the top of the first story with full length logs, the cross ties installed. Note also planks were nailed to each log on either side of the door frame and the door opening was cut out with a chain saw.

Photo 5 shows the cross ties on the top of the first story from the outside.

Photo 6 shows the cross ties looking up from inside of the first story. A sub floor was then laid on these logs which also formed the ceiling for the first story.

Photo 7 shows the cabin wall built up five more logs above the upper floor. The ridge board is held in place by two permanent, upright support braces and some temporary supports.

Photos 8, 9, and 10 show the installation of the roof rafters. The top wall log and the lower end of the rafters are both notched to join near perfectly. This is done to assure an even surface for accepting the roof boards. Note opening in rafters where dormer is to be built overlooking the West Fork of the Dolores River and the trail to the Geyser and Geyser Park.

Photos 11 and 12 show the roof boards being nailed to the roof rafters.

109

Photo 13 (above) shows the roof boards being covered with tar paper to protect them from the weather while the other side of the roof is being completed. Photo 14 (right) shows the cabin with all the roof boards in place and the dormer completed. The roof was then covered with tar paper. This photo also shows the workmen installing the metal sheets of roofing. Photo 15 (below) shows the cabin ready for winter use. The cracks between the logs are chinked with a special mixture of concrete for the climate at the cabin site.

Cache

This type of cache was designed by trappers and woodsmen to protect their furs and meat from marauding wildlife. This cache, although designed for the woodsman, works well as a substitute for a treehouse for the homeowner to build as a children's playhouse. This type of playhouse has the added advantage of not damaging your valuable ornamental shade trees. It is also much safer for your children.

1. Assemble the two sets of logs for legs with framing for each side, including main deck stringers.
2. Raise and stand one set of legs using temporary bracing poles stuck in the ground and spiked to the legs.
3. Raise and brace the second set of legs.
4. Brace the first and second sets of legs together with cross bracing.
5. Install the floor cross members.
6. Install the cache's deck.
7. Build the two side walls, the back and front walls of the cabin part of the cache.

The weight of the logs and the amount of help you have will be the determining factors on whether you build these sides on the ground or up on the deck of the cache.

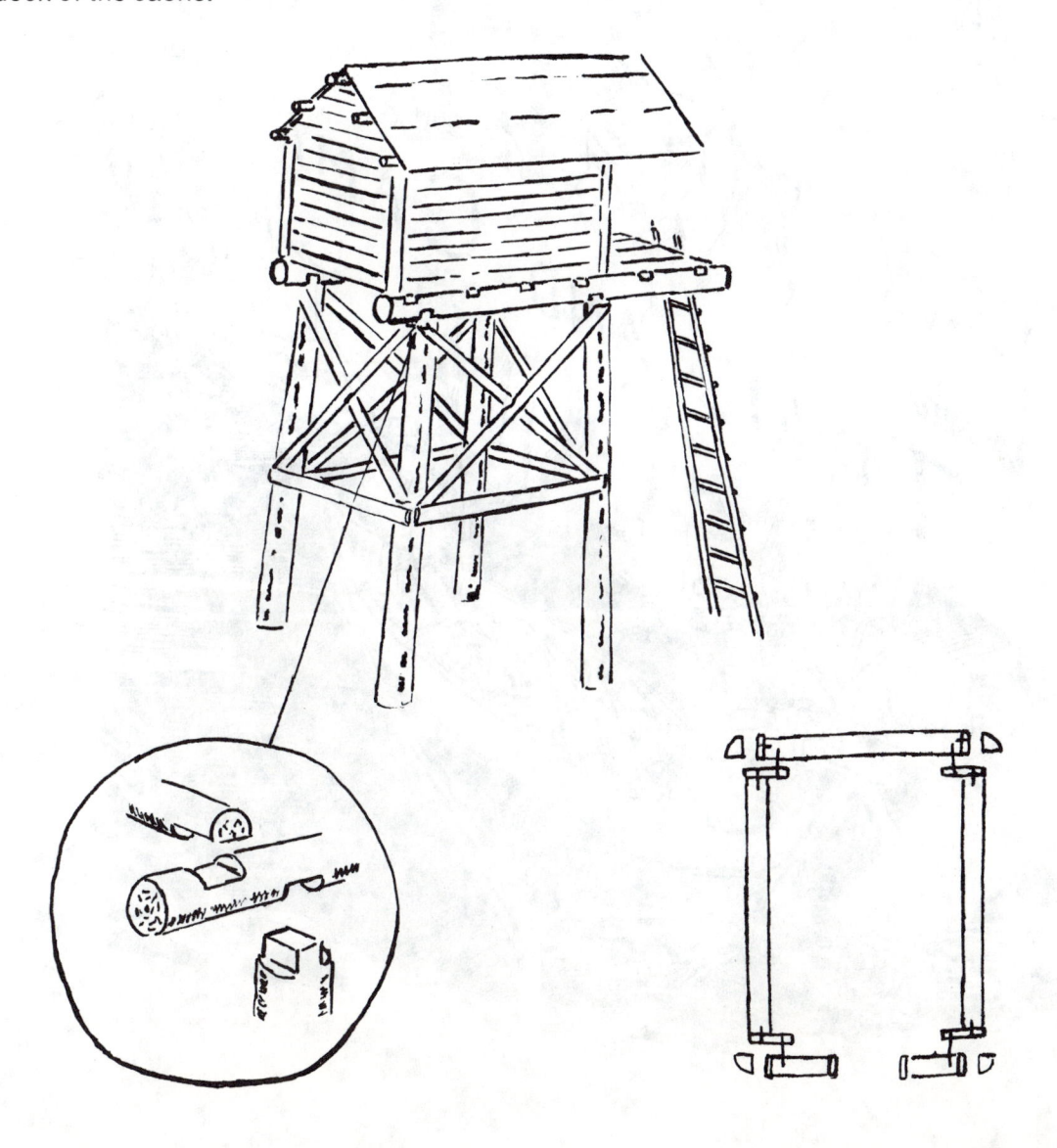

111

TRAIL AND CAMP

7.
Trail and Camp

Chain saws for use on the trail and in camp can be one of the best outdoor sports investments ever made for the hunter or fisherman. They can save you priceless hours in clearing a trail or obtaining firewood. The noise they make is soon forgotten by man and wildlife when you consider the extra days you will have to hunt or fish by not having to struggle with a hand saw or axe. However, never leave your axe at home. You will need it to split wood, perhaps to cut bone and there is always the possibility you will run out of saw gas or have some other misfortune with your chain saw. On the other hand, you might break your axe handle.

Once in a while a guy will hike into a wilderness lake to go fishing, and to study the area for hunting season. When he gets there all the fish seem to be jumping in the middle of the lake. If he brought his chain saw he could fashion a raft or some other sort of water craft. There are two rafts illustrated in this chapter, each of which can be built in less than an hour. With his raft, the sportsman can not only get to where the fish are jumping, he can also explore the shores of the lake for wildlife without making noise by walking on the leaves. By observing this wildlife, he can enrich his trip a hundredfold.

Last year during elk and deer bow hunting season, I set up a small camp for myself and my two hunting horses. In this area I had seen many bull elk and called my brother-in-law who also happens to be my favorite hunting partner. He told me that he would be here for rifle season and his son would be with him. I was working for the local electric power company at this time and had only one day off between bow and rifle season. There was a lot of blow down around my camp and along the trail. Using my chain saw and these blown down logs, I fashioned a solid lean-to type cabin that would withstand a pretty good storm. The cabin was easy to dismantle and disburse and left no more of a sign of man being there than any other part of the trail cleared for horse travel.

While I was building this structure, another sportsman came by with a chain saw. He was clearing the trail for his party's horses. They would be riding in during the dark hours the night before rifle season.

Toward the end of the season, there was a storm on the mountain we hunted. Again we had to cut the trail clear for our four legged hunting buddies. If we didn't have a chain saw in camp, I don't believe that we would have been able to get out of there before dark. It doesn't take a very big chain saw to out-perform an axe or hand saw.

If there should be any question on how to achieve the projects with your chain saw, please refer to the appropriate page in the How-to chapter.

Tent Frame

Camp Table

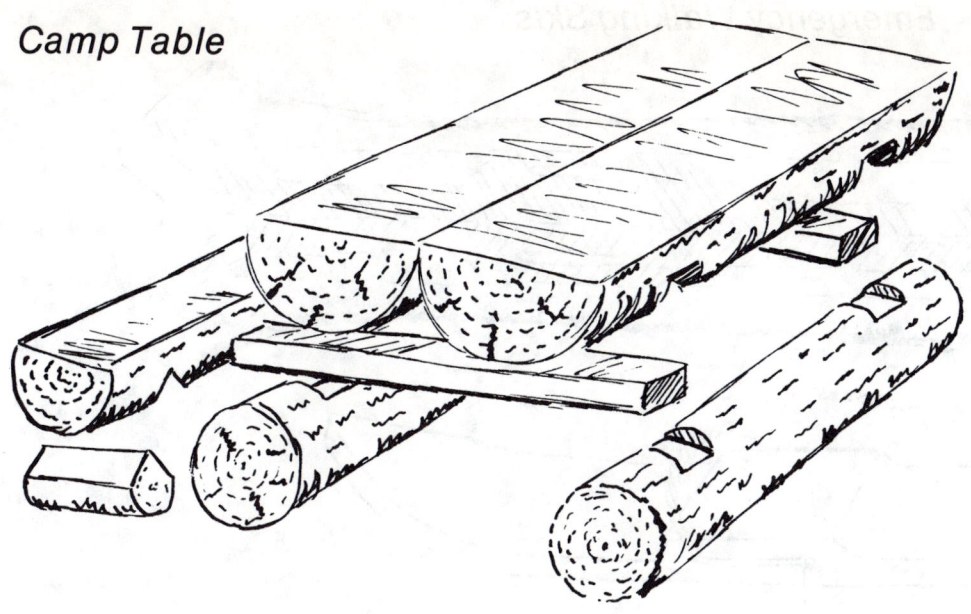

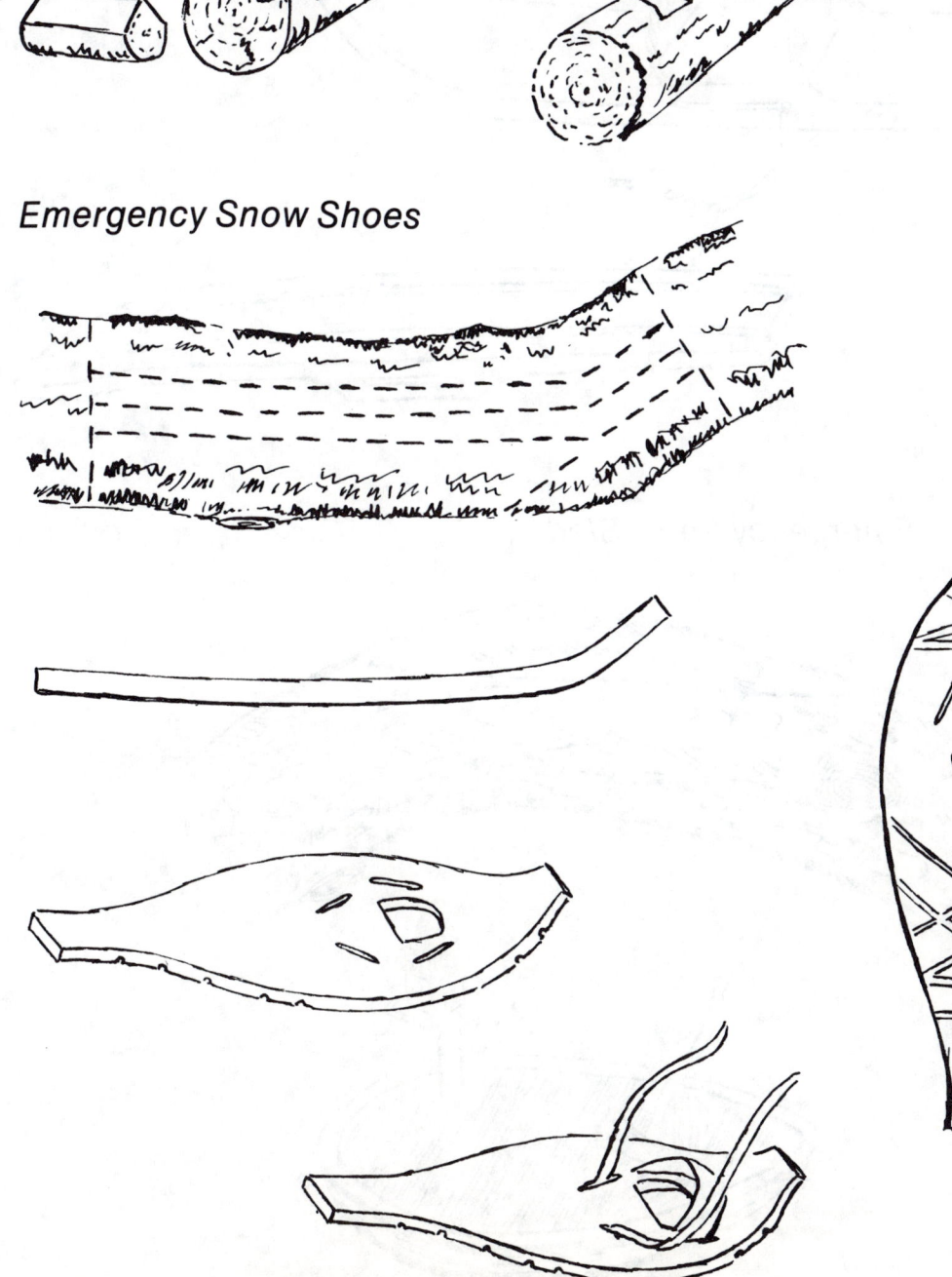

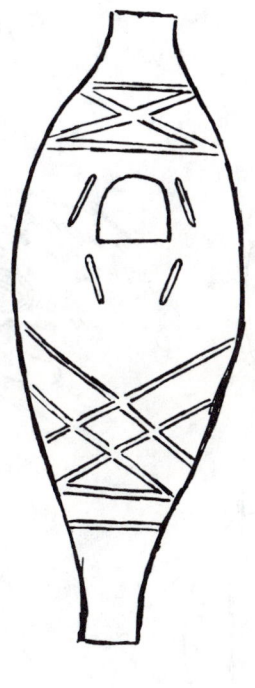

Emergency Snow Shoes

Emergency Walking Skis

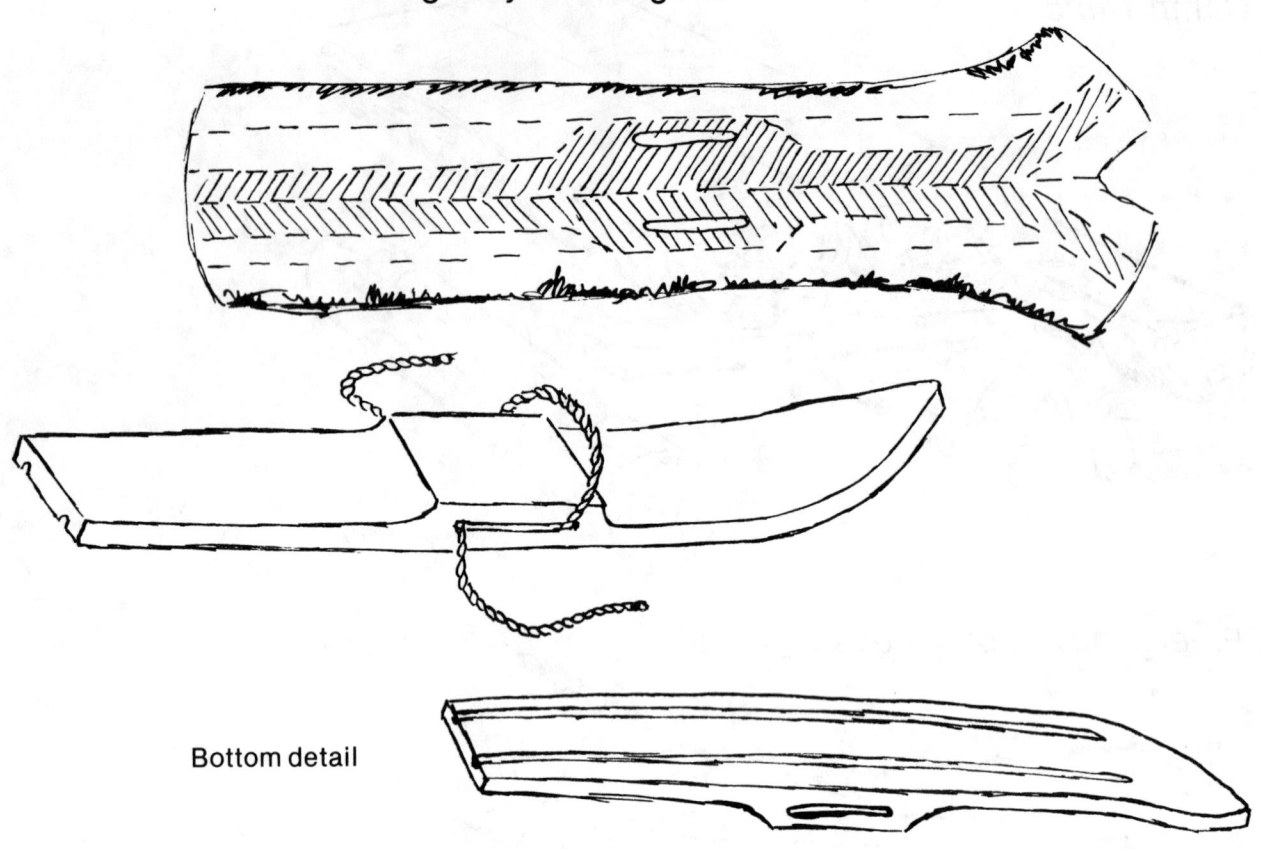

Bottom detail

Emergency Snow Sled

Completed Snow Sled

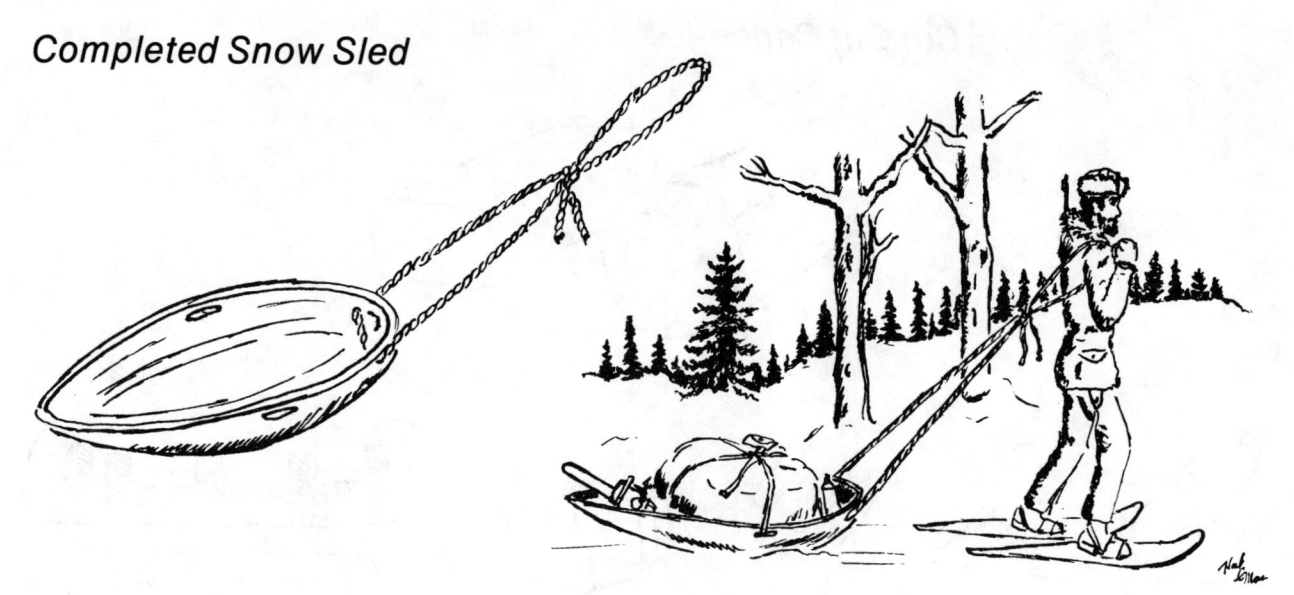

Hollowed Out Canoe

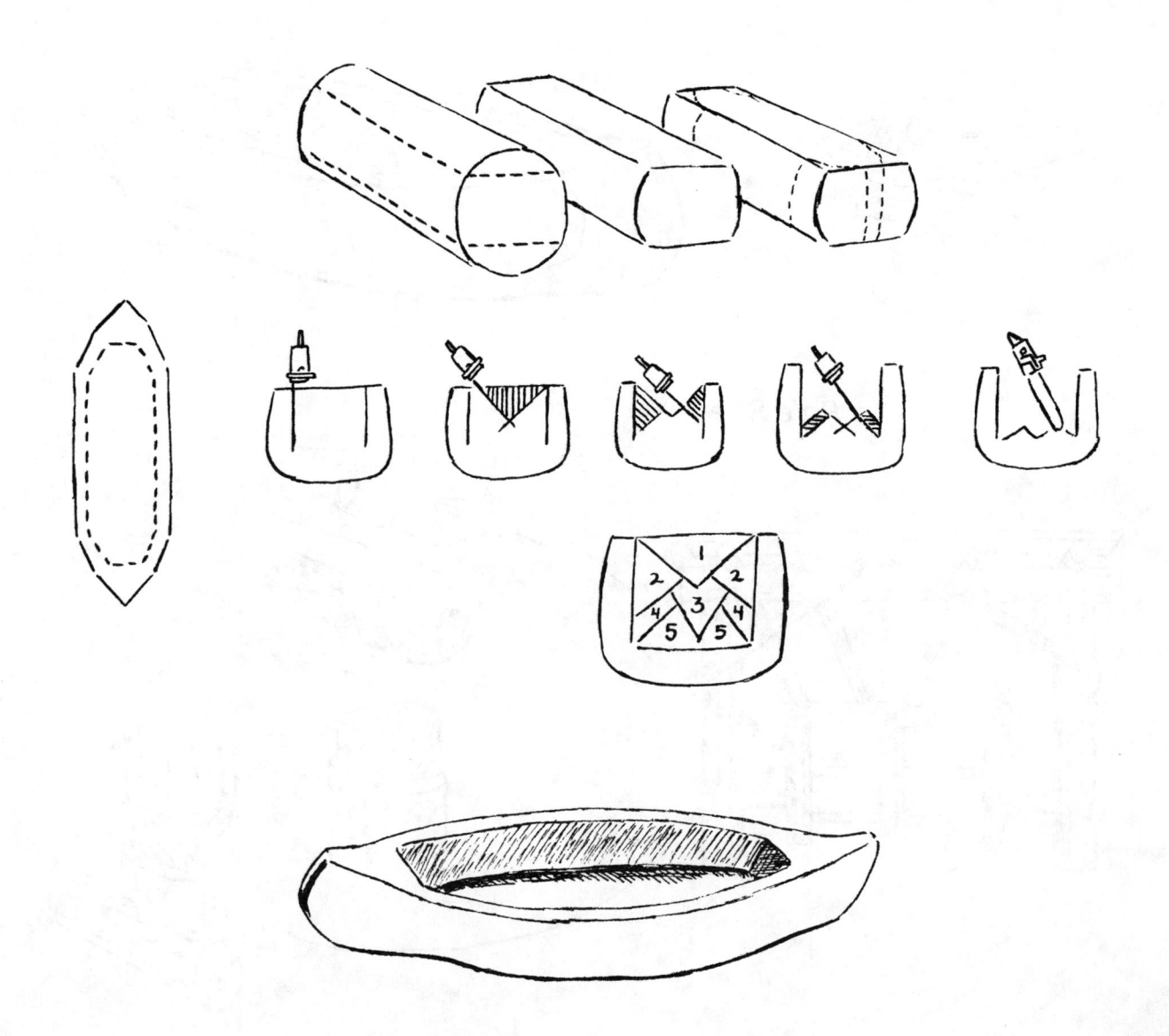

117

Cut Out Canoe

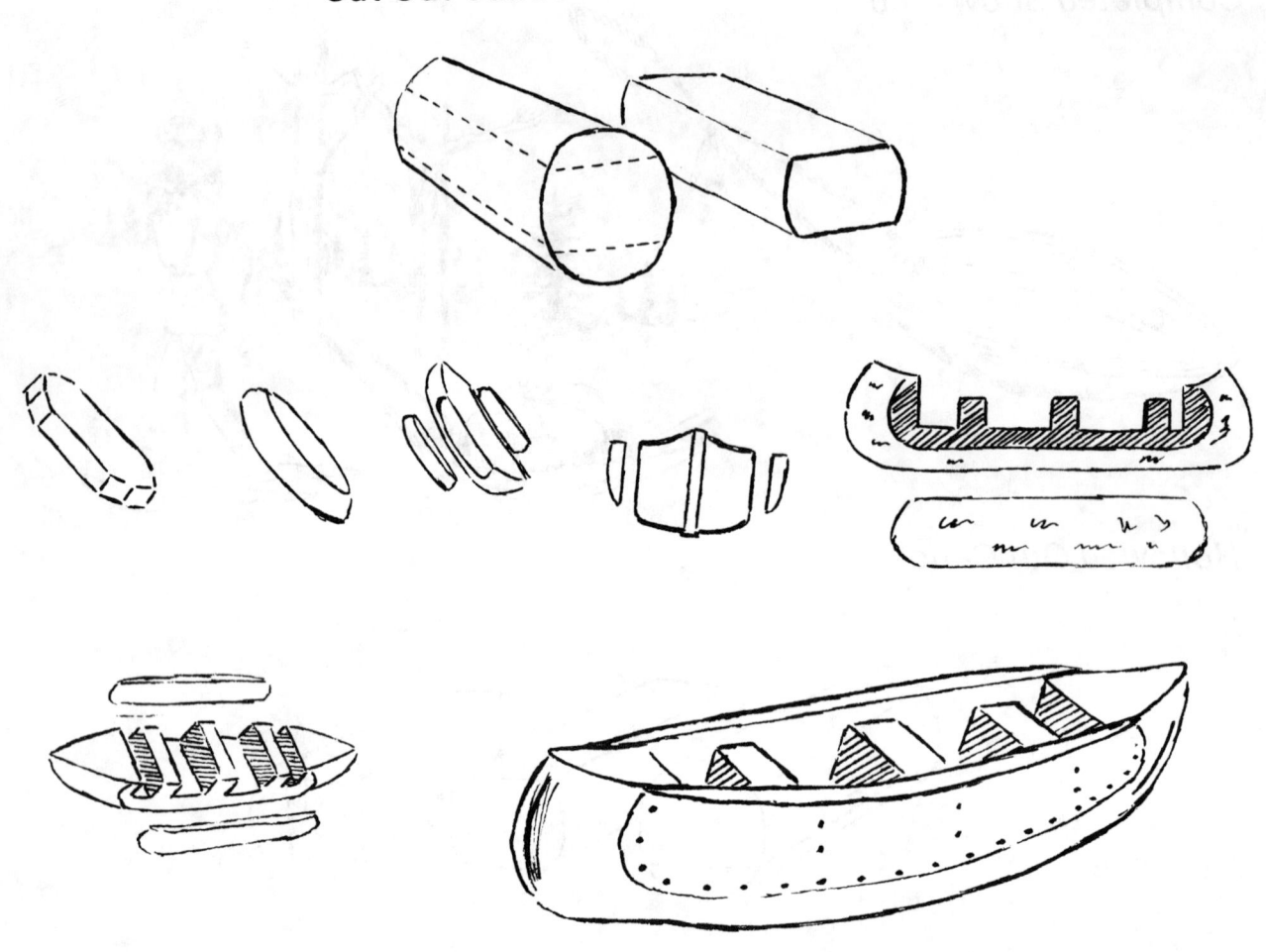

Pole Shed

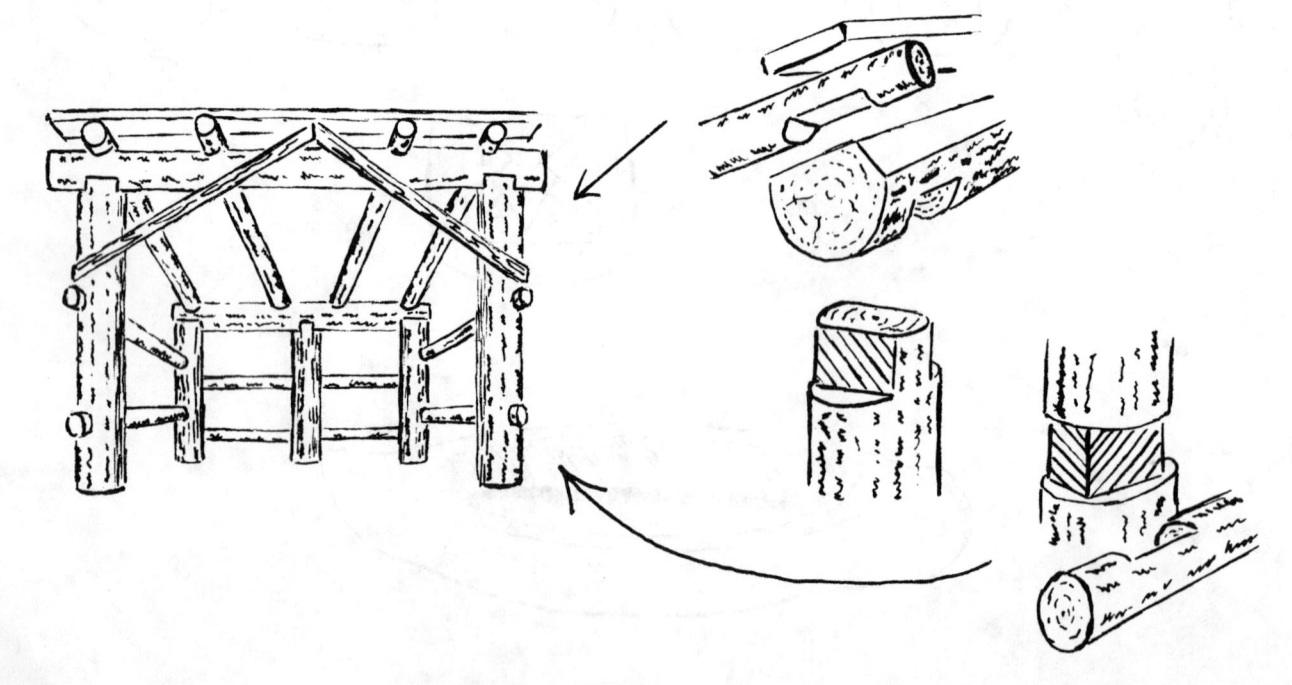

118

Two Simple Rafts

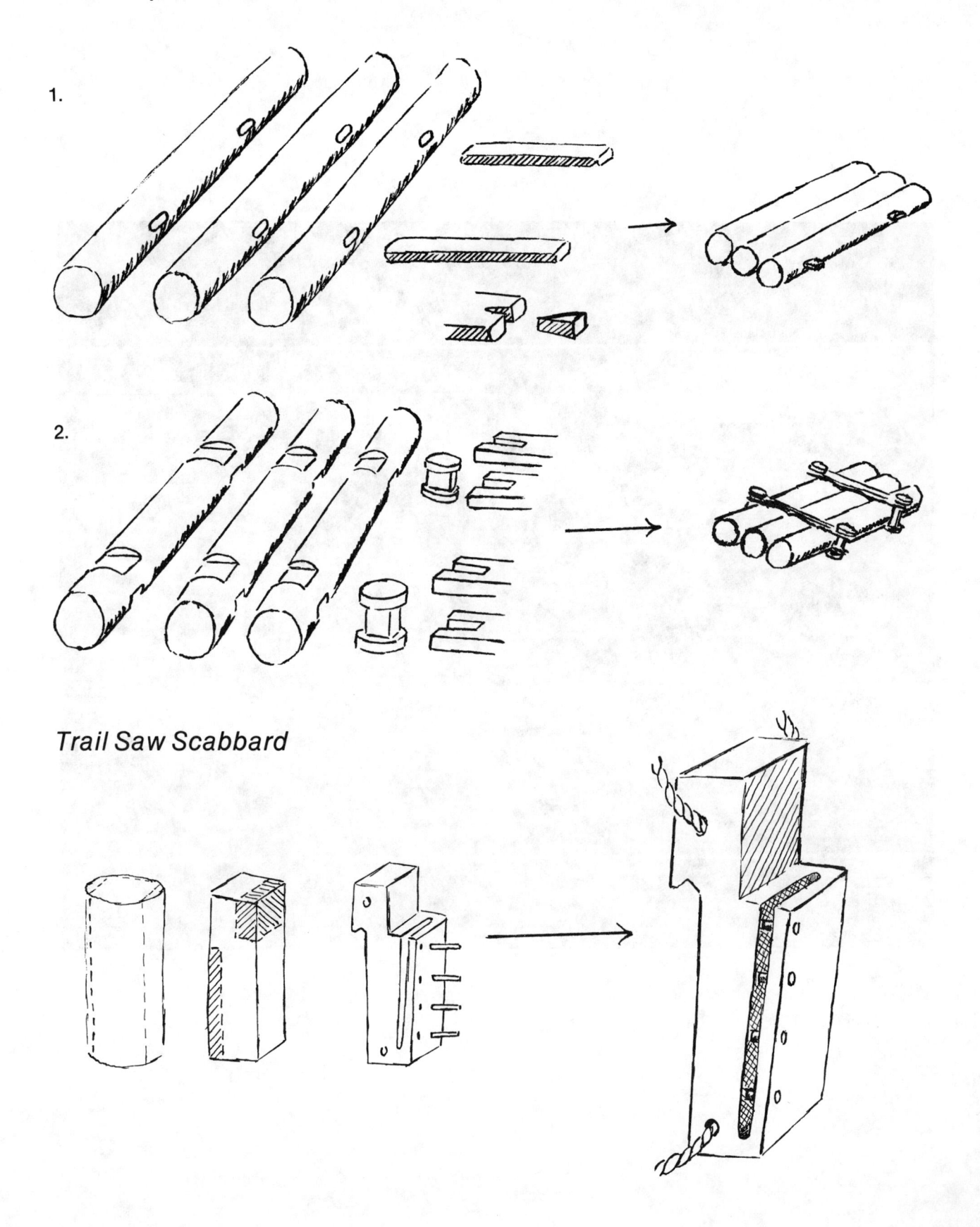

1.

2.

Trail Saw Scabbard

119

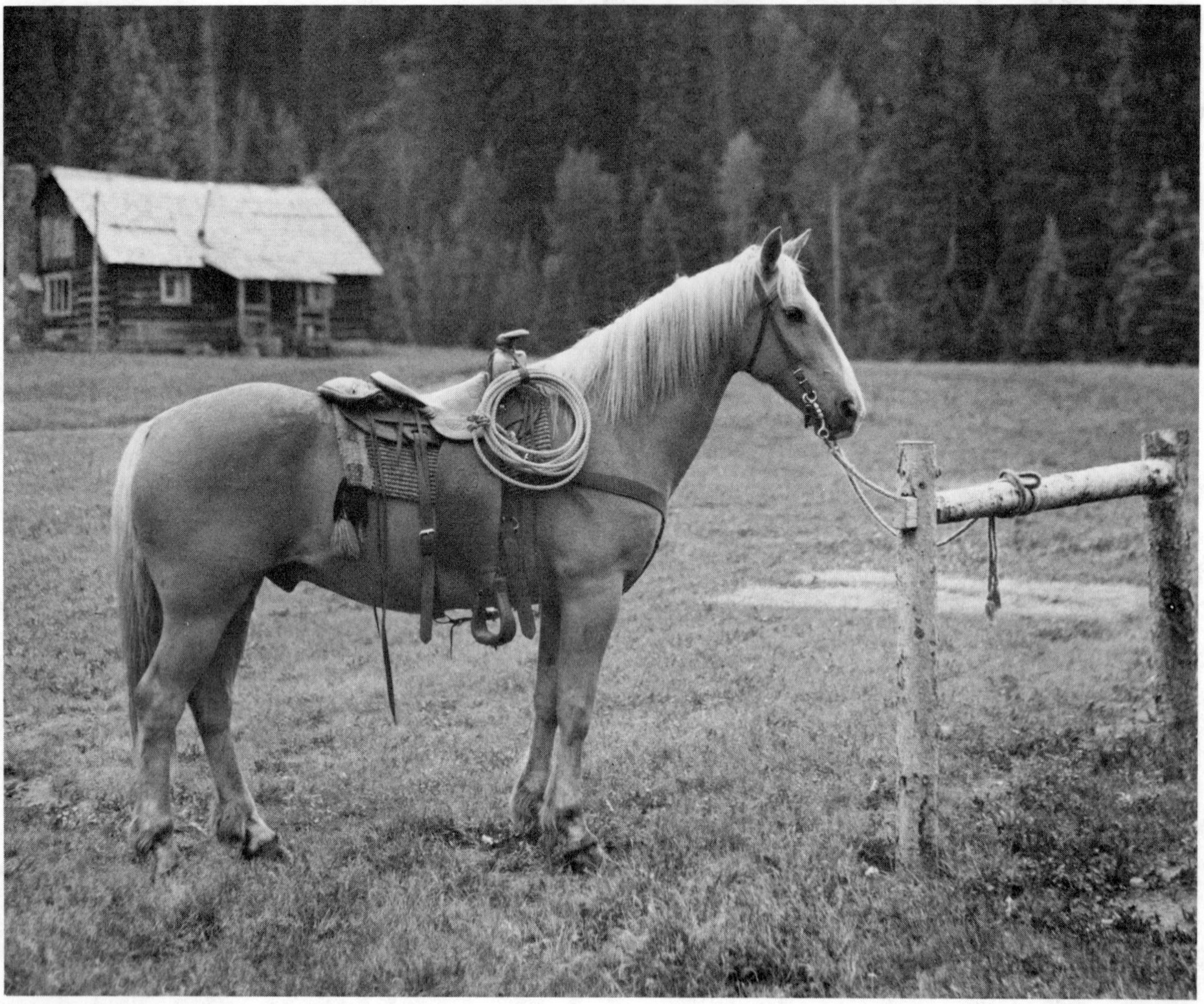

8.
Farm and Ranch

This chapter is mainly for those folks who have purchased chain saws for pruning orchards, wood lot improvement and removing dead trees. I hope to share with them a few ideas they may not have considered to regain their investment in their chain saw.

Constructing pole buildings for stock sheds, machinery storage, etc., are one of the cheapest and fastest shelters to construct. They are also a great protection for your other investments. I have only illustrated one pole building in this chapter, but think that with this one design, plus the information included in the section entitled Log Structures, there will be enough information for you to plan and build the necessary pole buildings for your needs.

The rail fences illustrated and photographed in this chapter make good use of trees cut for establishing property boundaries. They keep stock in their intended area, while not being a hazard or a restriction to deer, elk, and antelope. A small chain saw can also save countless hours per year in fence repair.

There are hundreds of other uses for chain saws on the farm and ranch, in addition to the ones I will discuss here. One common use is splitting slaughtered, skinned livestock. Of course, the chain oiler is washed out first, then replaced with thick, clean, cooking oil. When used for butchering, the entire saw must be as clean as your kitchen's electric mixer.

Hitching Post

Commonly Built Fences

1.

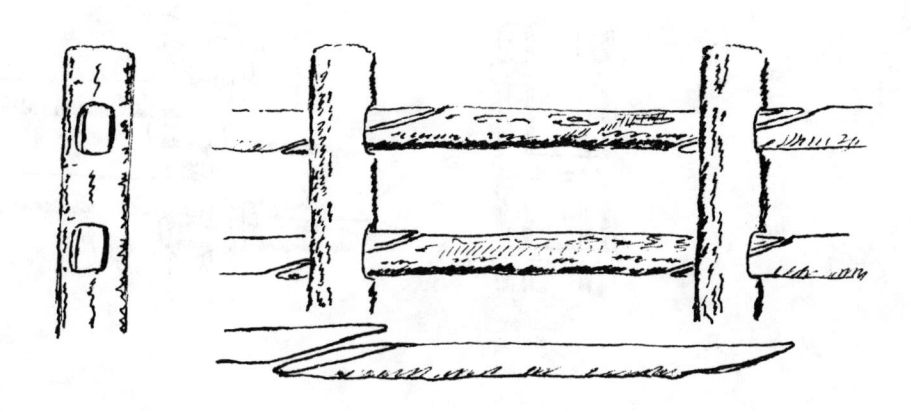

2.

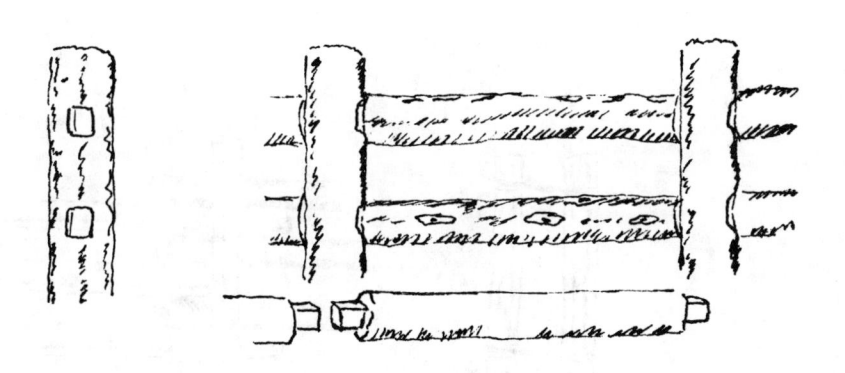

3.

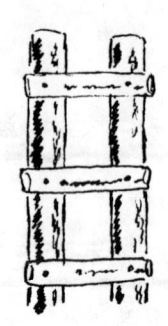

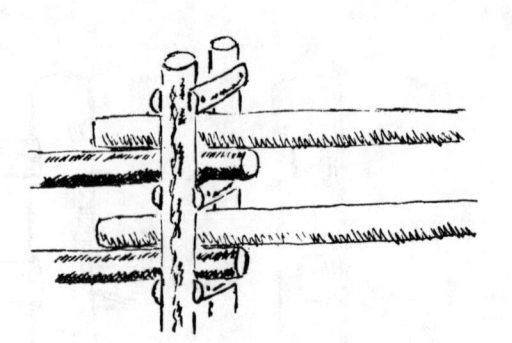

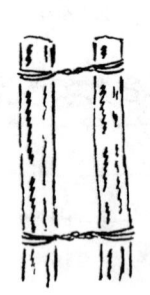

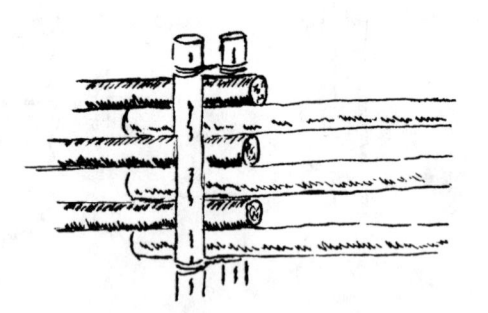

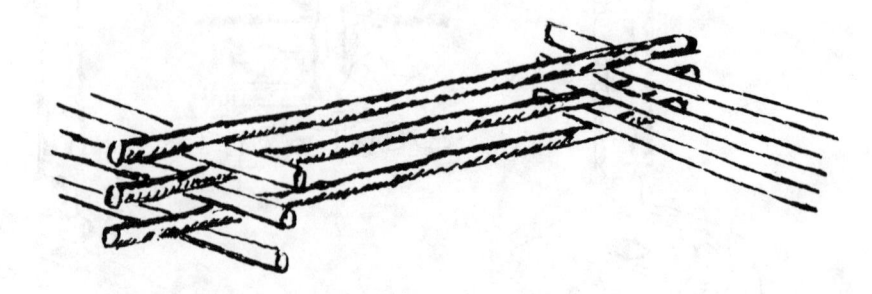

4.

5.

6.

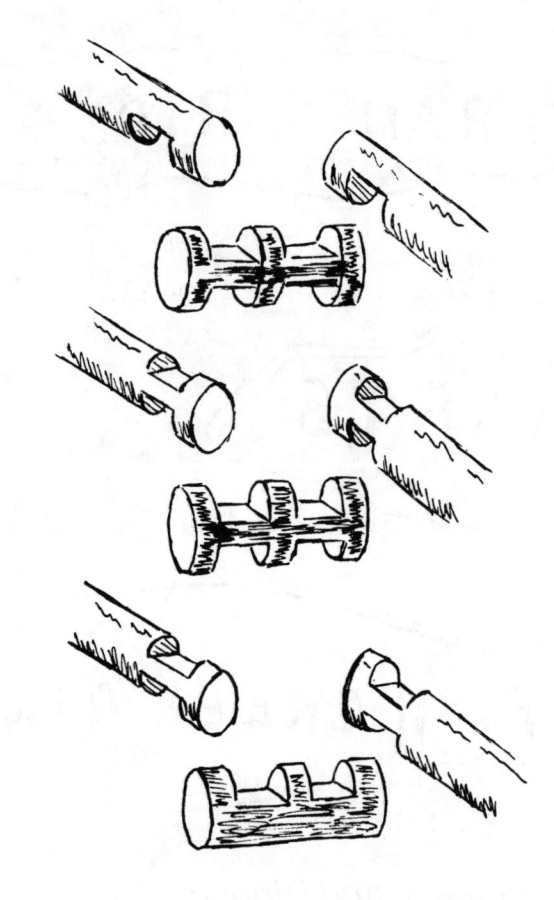

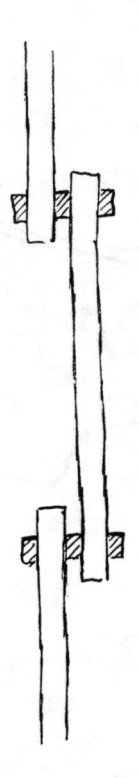

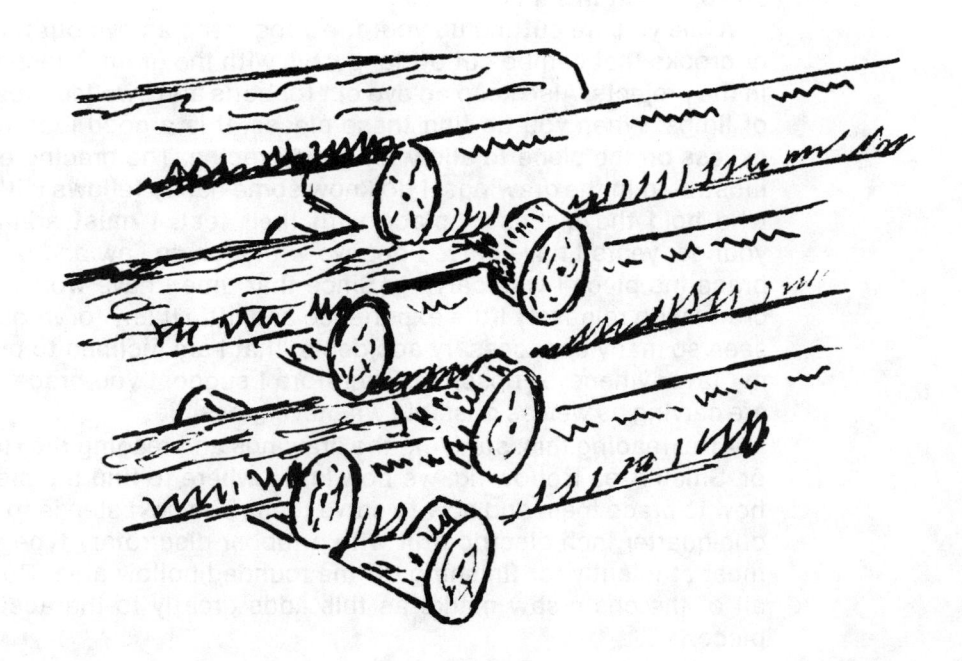

7.

8.

Sign Ideas

TRAIL RIDES

CABIN CRAFTS

FISH CREEK RANCH

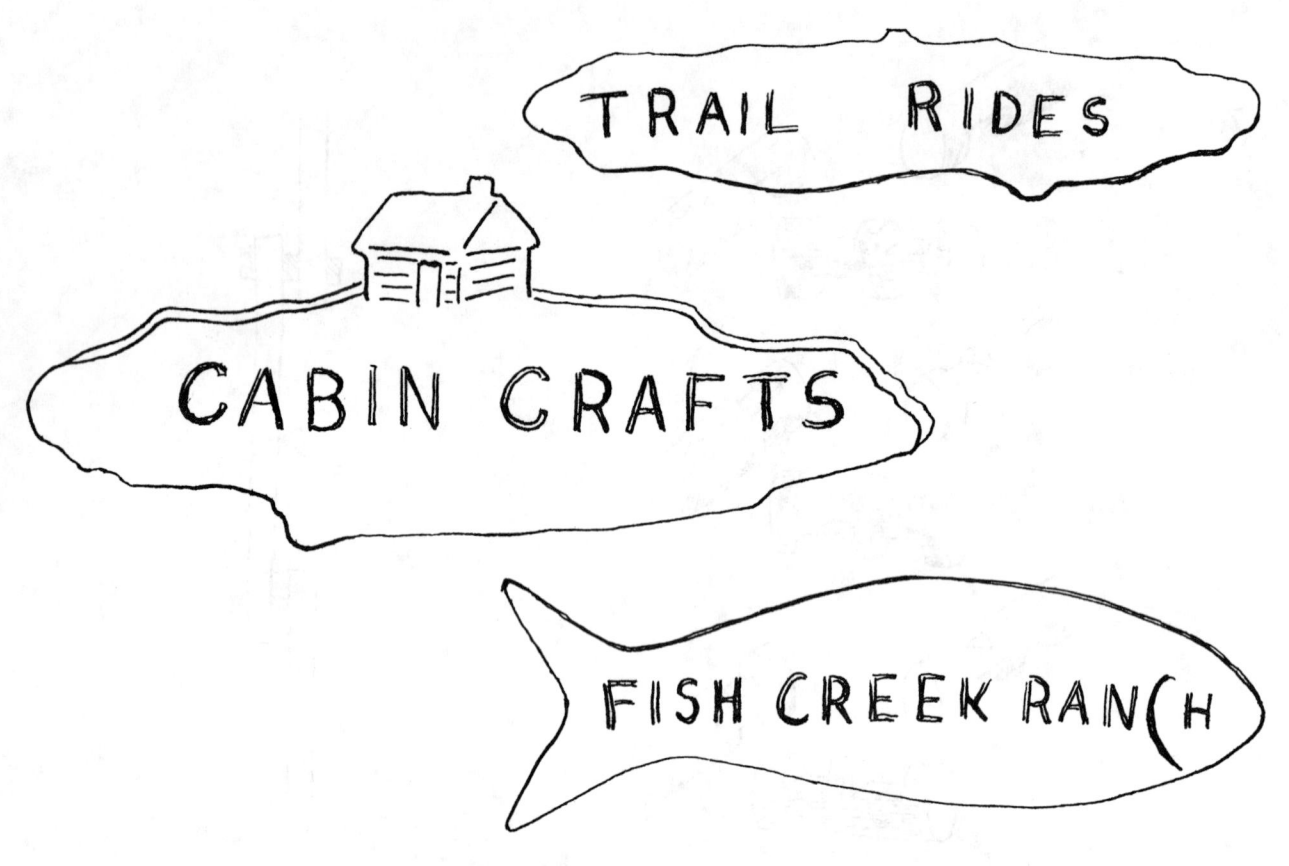

Carving Bowls, Baskets, and Dippers

The process of carving bowls, baskets and dippers is sufficienty covered in the How-to section on Small Area Hollowing. However, there are so many useful and attractive items that you can make in this manner I will add a little at this time.

While you are cutting up your firewood, keep an eye out for sharp bends or crooks that can be cut off longways with the grain. These will be useful in the projects. Also keep an eye out for burls and swelled areas at the base of limbs. When you do find these pieces, it is a good idea to leave some excess on the piece to allow for good bracing. The bracing excess is well illustrated in the drawings. I do know some handy fellows with a chain saw who hold the pieces in place with their feet. I must admit that in my younger years I have carved decoys with a chain saw and used my feet to brace the piece I was carving. Since that time I have worked on so many crews with relatively little experience and little if any forethought and have seen so many unnecessary accidents, that I am inclined to put the odds in my favor whenever possible. Therefore I suggest you brace whatever you are carving as well as possible whenever possible.

After reading this, studying the drawings and reading the How-to section on Small Area Hollowing, we now know where to find the pieces to carve, how to brace them and how to carve them. The next step is to sand them. A one-quarter inch electric drill with a rubber disc rotary type sander works most efficiently for finishing off the rounded hollow area. Do not sand out all of the chain saw marks as this adds greatly to the aesthetics of the piece.

Finding interesting pieces of wood for bowls, dippers and baskets.

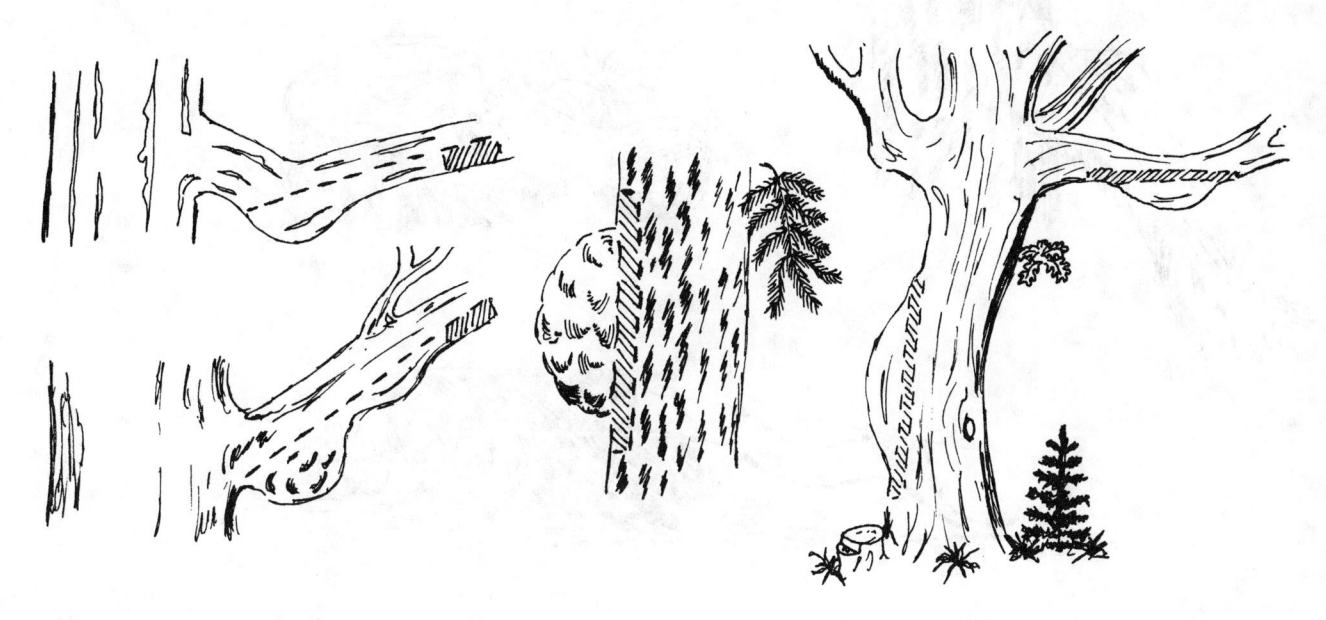

Bracing Techniques

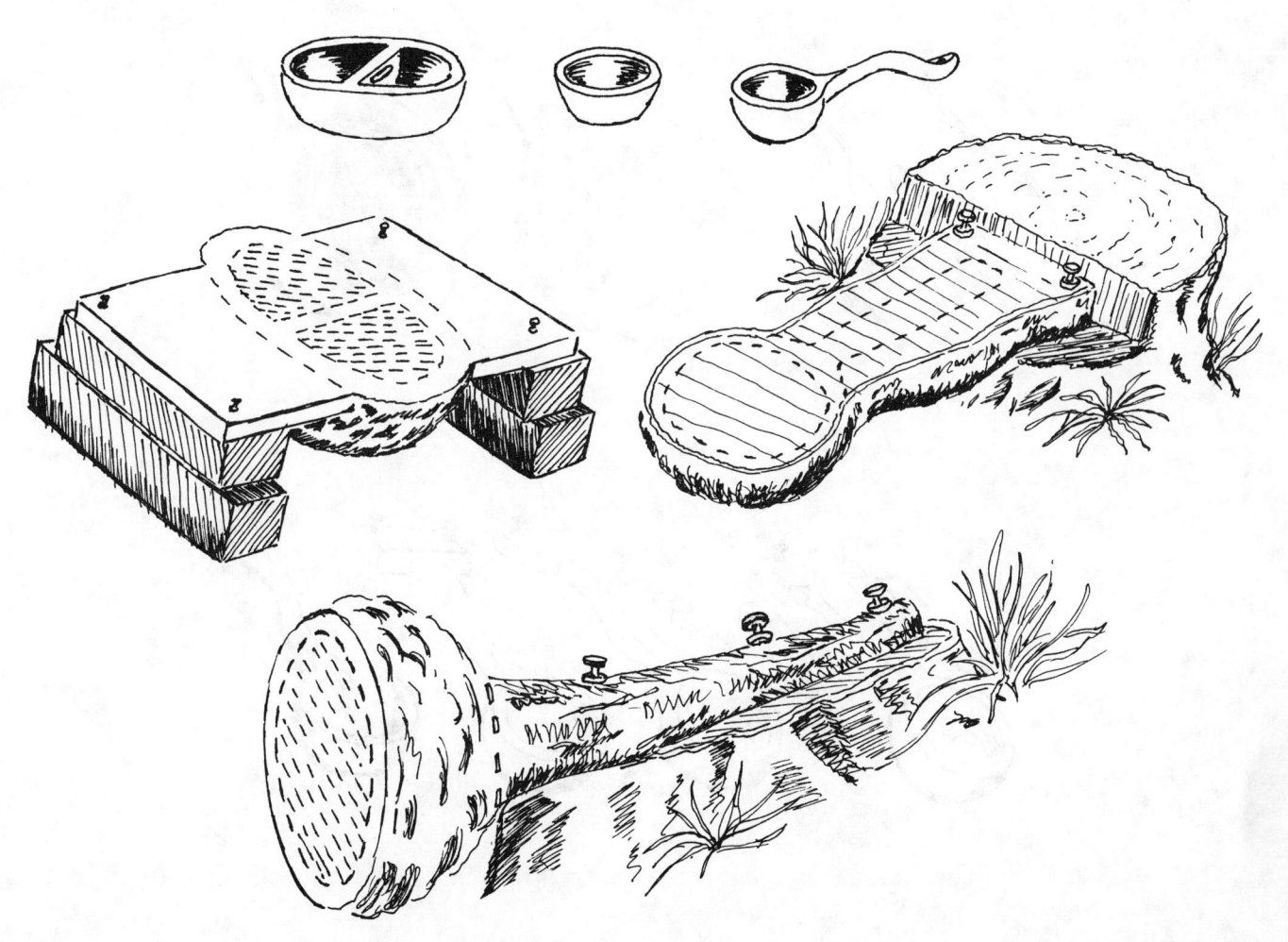

127

Dippers

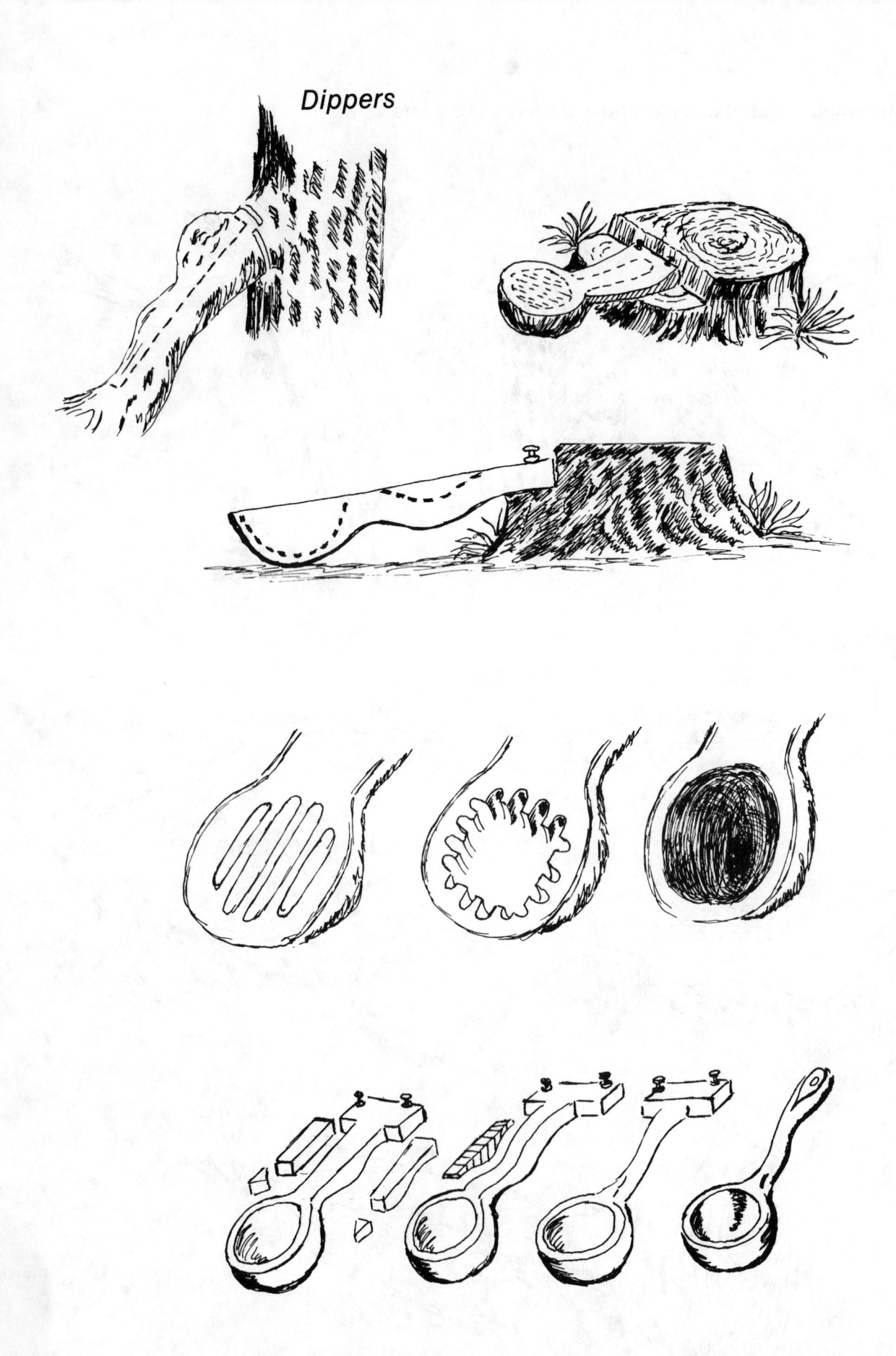

Hollowing Bowls and Baskets

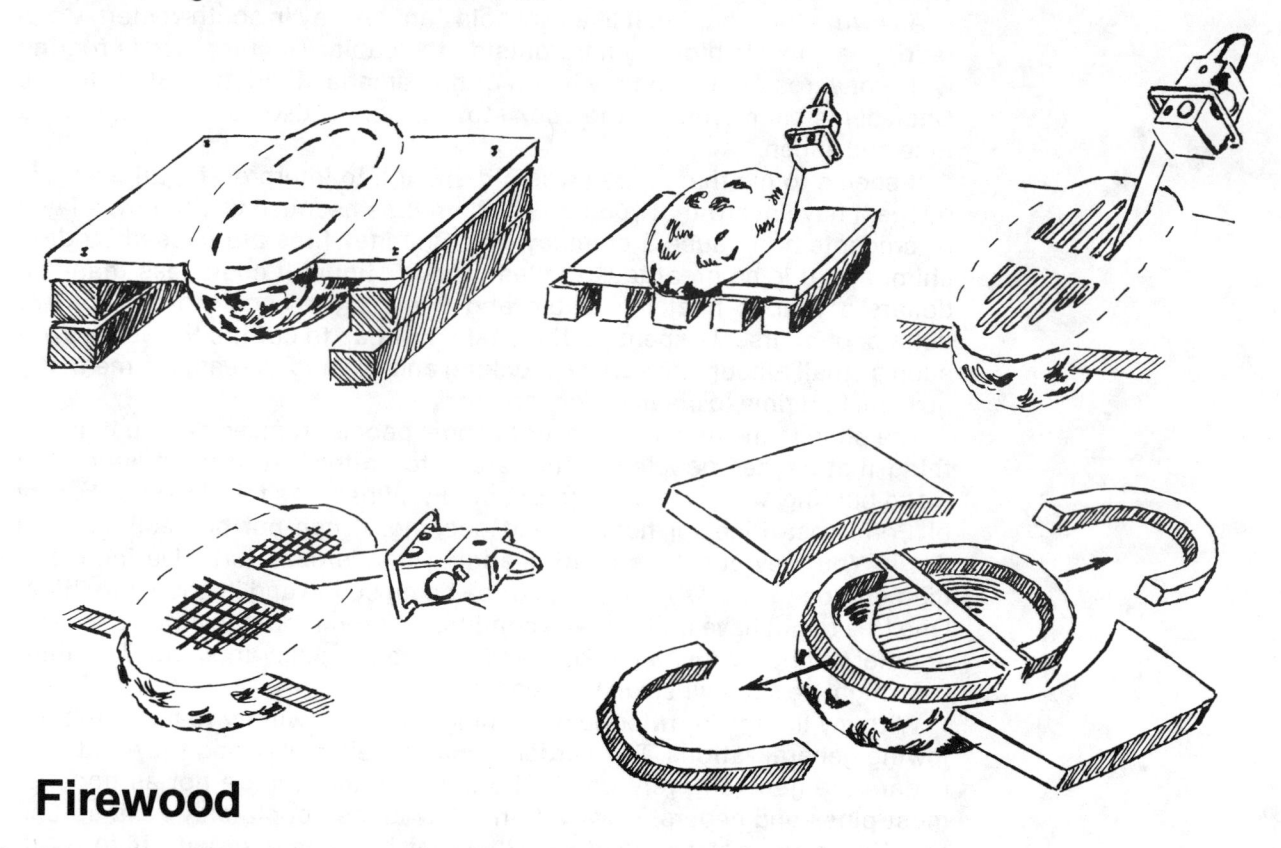

Firewood

For Fireplace and Cook Stove

Most everyone that has ever used a fireplace believes that most deciduous trees are good firewood and most conifers are not. If you live in an area where there is an overabundance of hardwood forests, chances are you will only burn a variety of oaks, maples, ashes, hickories and other harder deciduous trees.

I doubt that you or any firewood salesman would take the time to mess with the poplar family or the willow family, as they are more difficult to age than the harder deciduous trees. Not many people use such soft deciduous trees as catalpa, basswood, linden or sassafras whenever harder trees are available. In areas where hard deciduous trees abound, it is often believed that the entire poplar family is useless for firewood. This is not so. A large, standing, dead and dry poplar makes very fine firewood. In the Rockies, the aspen is one of the most favored firewoods. If you cut the standing dead tree it will give off a great amount of heat and will last sufficiently long in a cook stove. For use in the fireplace or wood-heating stove, aspen is also quite good. For a long lasting fire of aspen, start the fire with dry wood. After the fire is burning satisfactorily, add some one-third green wood or one-half green wood. The partly green or unaged wood will simmer many hours.

Another deciduous tree that has a poor reputation for firewood is the American Elm. The main reason is that it is so hard to split. If you can split it small enough for your fireplace, it makes great firewood. One caution here, if the tree has been killed by Dutch Elm Disease when the wood is burned, the disease will spread throughout your neighborhood. In much the same manner that burning poison ivy would spread onto people where you burn it, the elm disease will spread to the nearby elm trees.

Burning Conifers

As I write this chapter, it is a very cold January day in southwestern Colorado. The snow is blowing hard outside the cabin. The fireplace is roaring with Ponderosa Pine, and my lunch of homemade Manhattan Blue Grouse Chowder is simmering on the cook stove which is also burning Ponderosa Pine and aspen.

It seems to me that since I was old enough to interpret the English language, I have heard that you can not burn pine because it will form a layer of creosote and cause a chimney fire. Chimney fires are caused by dirty chimneys. It is no great task to clean them. I figure it costs less than five dollars a year to heat this cabin and operate the cook stove. This five dollars, of course, is spent on the chain saw gas to cut the firewood. With such a small amount invested in cooking and heating, it seems to me that a guy can find time to clean his chimney.

The pitch in the pine that prevents some people from ever using it, is the thing that causes people in other areas to prefer it. The pitch keeps the wood burning and gives off a great amount of heat. As for the exact quality of Ponderosa Pine for heating and cooking, it can not be easily pinned down. You may cut three dead, standing Ponderosas forty-five inches in diameter on the same hillside. All three being sound and in good condition. One tree might have uniform sap conditions throughout the entire tree, and another might have sap pockets and be slightly pulpy in spots. The third tree might be somewhere in between.

With my limited knowledge of burning conifers I will try to make the following generalizations. The harder pines are relatively good firewood. The cedars are generally very good. The spruces and firs are not as good as most pines and cedars. However, in many areas people only have spruce and firs to use for firewood and they get by quite well with it for both cooking and heating.

Even if you are fortunate enough to live in an area that abounds in good hardwoods for firewood (ash, beech, maple, and oak, etc.), you should still not completely disregard the conifers and the poplar family. These trees make real good kindling and a good bed of coals for firing up your larger pieces of more valuable firewood.

Stocking up wood for the sole purpose of using it for the fireplace is something that takes a little consideration if you are to get the most for your effort. First of all, you should have three separate stacks of wood: kindling, starter wood, and heating wood. Kindling can be any easily combustible small wood, bark, cones, etc., that you have available. When splitting kindling it should generally be no greater than one inch at the thickest part. For my kindling, I use the chips, splinters, and bark left over from splitting of the larger pieces of firewood. Starting wood should be from two inches to six or eight inches in diameter, and very well seasoned. This will give you a good deal of flame and/or coals to start your larger heating wood. This wood can be less well seasoned and the diameter can be determined by the size of your fireplace and your physical health.

To me there seems to be some kind of magic in the cutting and hauling in of a winter supply of wood. If you are a sportsman, you will be trying to get most of your wood before hunting season and the first snow. The crisp autumn air mixes with nature's paintbrush. You have the feeling that you are joining nature in her ancient ways. The warm, providing feeling you have toward your household for performing this act of wood gathering makes the job very rewarding. Perhaps sometimes, to some people, it is hard, boring and tedious work. I can not recall of anyone complaining, but I have heard quite a few brags on the quantity and quality of wood obtained as well as a few arguments on the best wood to burn and the best chain saws to use. I believe the best wood is what grows nearby and the best chain saw is your own—because you are the one that takes care of it.

Firewood Selling

Here is what I consider to be one of the largest headaches if you are planning to start a small firewood business. Many of your customers will want sissy wood. This is wood sixteen inches long and four inches in diameter or less at the widest point. This wood is great for getting a fire started, but it burns up too fast. People that split their own firewood have a tendency to burn chunks of wood that just fit the fireplace or are just light enough to carry without getting a hernia. I once had a customer in upstate New York that wanted three face cords of wood split to two inches in diameter plus he wanted a one-half face cord of kindling. The time consumed in preparing such a delivery would have left me with about twenty cents an hour, if that, after delivering and restacking the wood at the customer's house.

The only way to prevent losing money and time and prevent poor public relations is to be sure your customer knows exactly what you have and for you to know exactly what he wants. Tell him the species of trees that will be included in his order, how long they have been aged, the range of diameters of the pieces of wood he will receive, the length the sticks will be, and the dimensions of your face cords.

One of the trickiest and most frustrating things to both you and your customer, if not discussed beforehand, is what happens to the wood at the point of delivery. Number one, do you just dump it in the yard, driveway or backyard? Will the driveway support your truck without causing a lawsuit? Will you have to stack the wood and, if so, how far will this stacking point be from where you can drive? Whether you dump the wood in one minute or spend four or five hours carrying it and stacking it in cellars should be a major consideration in giving the people a price. If you are going to advertise firewood for sale, most experienced firewood sellers' ads read like this: "Firewood For Sale—All Seasoned Hardwood. Face Cord Measuring Sixteen Inches By Four Feet By Eight Feet—$ _____." "Face Cord Measuring Twenty Inches By Four Feet By Eight Feet—$ _____." These prices are delivered and dumped, paid for before dumping. Some add a carrying and stacking price per man hour. If you are going to start a firewood business, I wish you the best of luck and may your God bless you. And don't forget to add up all your expenses and time involved, as compared with the local selling price for your wood.

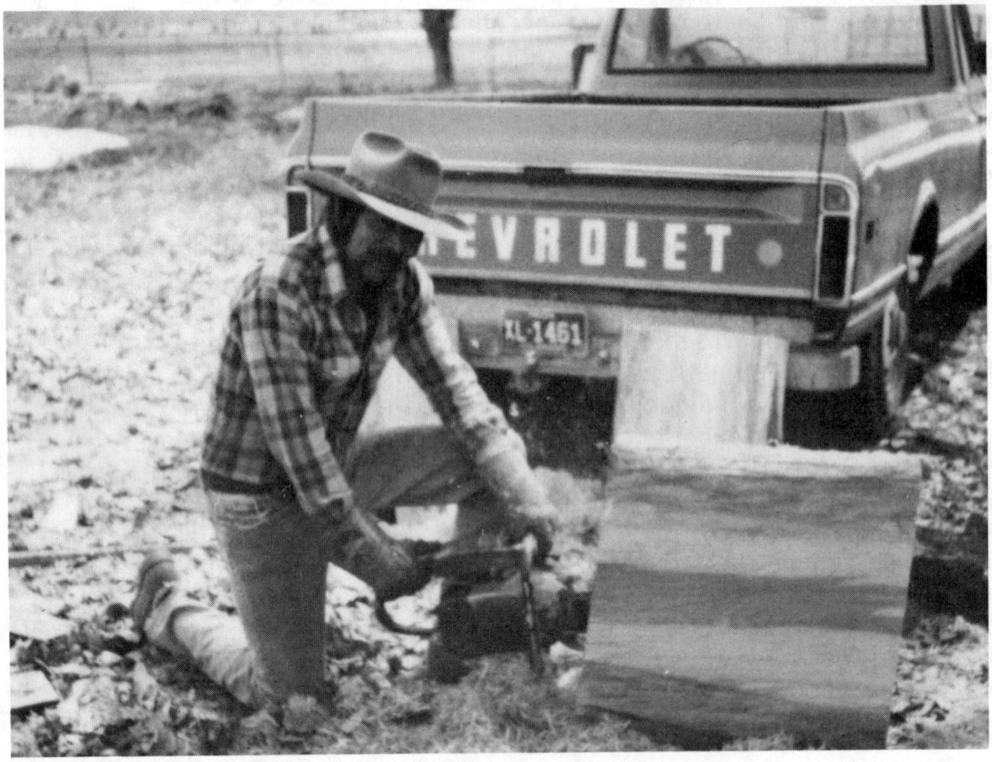
EVROLET
XL-1461

9.
The Author's Background With Chain Saws

Trimming power lines and removing dead trees in and over them is how I broke in as a tree climber many years ago, after I was discharged from the Marines. Most of my adult working life has been spent as a trimming line technician, performing tree surgery or as a tree expert. I have also done some logging. I suspect that as far as diversity in tree work goes, I am about as diversified as almost any tree man. I have removed trees in very restricted areas like the city of Albany, New York. Dead, rotten trees with stump diameters at one hundred and sixteen inches, sprawled over five buildings and umpteen power lines. I have roped down some of these trees and worked with eighty-five and one hundred and fifteen foot tree cranes on others. I have climbed with cranes and without them into the dark hours in emergency cases. I have worked quite a few ice storms in the Northeast. One time my compadres and I worked an ice storm seventy-two hours straight with wet boots and socks and frozen climbing and work ropes, trying to free tangled power lines. I have also ground a lot of stump, chipped a lot of brush and operated numerous tree loading devices.

The only reason I have mentioned any of this occupational experience is to let you know that with thousands of hours working in trees with a chain saw, chain saws are no more hazardous than pulling onto the street from your driveway. This is providing, of course, you are careful and respect your chain saw and use common sense as you do when you get into your auto.

I have two close friends that do not want to be near chain saws. They both cut their legs with chain saws, neither saw was running fortunately. They were merely not giving the saw or the starting instructions enough respect. Tree men start saws in cramped places that are sometimes covered with ice and wind blown while hanging onto a half inch rope. I myself feel safer doing this than I do driving down a Denver freeway in a trimlift. If you take the time to consider how well your saw can serve you, if you just give it a little respect and a firm hand, you will have little difficulty becoming its master or at least its friend.

As I write this book in a log cabin on the West Branch of the Dolores River in southwestern Colorado, I am keeping my feet warm by burning half green aspen wood in the fireplace. I am thinking back to hunting trips where we used chain saws to cut firewood in places like White Bear Lake in Newfoundland. There I carved my first goose decoys with a chain saw on a foggy day when it was too socked in to pursue moose and caribou. I think about a hunting camp on the Little Grays River in Wyoming and some great old guides that had their specific choices of the world's best chain saw. Of my friends in Sportsman's Club that won the National Wildlife Federation Award and the State Conservation Award with the aid of chain saws.

I think of my Dad, feeding the wood stove in his basement that heats his greenhouse, workshop, and winery. He is probably burning some dry ash, beech, oak, maple, a little birch and perhaps some American Elm knots. I understand that his wood stove in the basement cuts his home heating bill more than in half. I assume my Dad enjoys cutting and splitting his firewood. When his woodpile indoors gets low around December, he enjoys firing up his old Ford tractor with the bucket loader and snow chains and bringing in enough wood to last another month or so.

the Chain Saw Craft Book